BARACK OBAMA

ANTHONY PAINTER is a freelance political commentator who regularly contributes to the *Independent* and *Tribune*, and who also writes for a variety of other national publications. He was awarded the *New Statesman* prize for political writing in 2003 and will be a Labour candidate for the European Parliament in 2009. His blog can be read at www.anthonypainter.co.uk

BARACK OBAMA

The Movement for Change

ANTHONY PAINTER

Arcadia Books Ltd
15–16 Nassau Street
London W1W 7AB

www.arcadiabooks.com

First published by BlackAmber Inspirations
an imprint of Arcadia Books 2008

Series Editor: Rosemarie Hudson
Copyright © Anthony Painter 2008

ISBN 978-1-906413-23-1

Typeset in Minion by MacGuru Ltd
Printed and bound in England by CPI Cox & Wyman, Reading, Berkshire

Arcadia Books gratefully acknowledges the financial support of Arts Council England. Arcadia Books supports PEN, the fellowship of writers who work together to promote literature and its understanding. English PEN upholds writers' freedoms in Britain and around the world, challenging political and cultural limits on free expression.
To find out more, visit *www.englishpen.org* or contact
English PEN, 6–8 Amwell Street, London EC1R 1UQ

Arcadia Books distributors are as follows:

in the UK and elsewhere in Europe:
Turnaround Publishers Services
Unit 3, Olympia Trading Estate
Coburg Road
London N22 6TZ

in the USA and Canada:
Independent Publishers Group
814 N. Franklin Street
Chicago, IL 60610

in Australia:
Tower Books
PO Box 213
Brookvale, NSW 2100

in New Zealand:
Addenda
Box 78224
Grey Lynn
Auckland

in South Africa:
Quartet Sales and Marketing
PO Box 1218
Northcliffe
Johannesburg 2115

Arcadia Books: *Sunday Times* Small Publisher of the Year 2002/03

Contents

	Introduction	1
1	Race, Poverty and Ho Chi Minh	20
2	Backlash	54
3	Chicago	76
4	Harold Washington	115
5	Obama's Rise	138
6	Becoming President	170
	Conclusion	193
	Biographical Notes	199
	Acknowledgements	207
	Bibliography	210

To my family: Chris, Norah, Jennifer, Joe, George and Claire, an inspiration, not here but always near.

Introduction

MILE HIGH STADIUM IN DENVER, home to the Broncos, is better known for feats of sporting prowess than moments of national history. Yet on August 28, 2008, an African-American*, from Hawaii, with a white mother from Kansas and a father from Alego in Kenya, stood before 80,000 people and accepted the nomination of the Democratic Party for President of the United States of America.

Eighteen months previously, on February 10, 2007, on a bitingly cold day before the Old State Capitol Building in Springfield, Illinois, 17,000 people watched

---

*Ethnicity is a slippery concept and a difficult one to nail down satisfactorily. As a matter of fact, Barack Obama is a mixed-race American but clearly identifies himself as African-American. Not wanting to get into a fruitless debate about ethnic definition as it is thankless, I am happy to go along with that so describe him as both mixed-race and African-American depending on the context.

Barack Obama announce that he was running for the presidency of the United States. On the same site, nearly 150 years previously, Abraham Lincoln, another gangly, articulate lawyer from Illinois, running against a more experienced field of opponents for the nomination of the Republican party, had declared: 'A house divided against itself cannot stand. I believe this government cannot endure, permanently, half-slave and half-free. I do not expect the Union to be dissolved – I do not expect the house to fall – but I do expect it will cease to be divided.'

Along with Franklin Delano Roosevelt, Abraham Lincoln would go on to be the most brilliant President of the post-founding fathers. When he gave that address few would have thought that standing before them was the man who would, through an Emancipation Proclamation, abolish slavery, Britain's sordid imperial bequest to America that became the Republic's original sin. Likewise, a few dreamers, a few who were in the mood to follow faith rather than hard-headed realism, a few who knew Senator Obama, and perhaps, just as importantly, knew what type of campaign they had on the stocks, believed that this charismatic, effervescent, self-assured politician would just eighteen months later become the first African-American to accept his party's nomination and a few months later President of the United States.

Close followers of the American political scene knew of Barack Obama in February 2007. By that August day in Denver eighteen months later, the whole world had heard of him. Most were inspired. Many couldn't quite believe what was happening, either shying away or just simply succumbing to the mood, the opportunity, the momentum. Others played their resentful, unforgiving, historical role. Others liked the man but not his politics or just preferred their girl, Hillary. Whatever the reaction, Barack Obama was the story, the illuminating light that insisted upon the world's gaze, and then demanded its whole-hearted and unflinching focus. He was the questioning of every assumption, a candidate with greater meaning than even the presidential race itself, a one-man frontier, not simply a new chapter but an entirely new story. Here was change that could be believed in, change that, in the blink of an eye, the flick of a camera shutter, the flash of a spotlight, was his story, America's latest epic – a new twenty-first century folklore.

As he embarked on his precocious journey, mild scepticism could be forgiven. In terms of tone, the bi-partisan message resonated, and in his raw ability to communicate, Barack Obama was an altogether more exciting politician than had been seen for quite some time. He was up against the Clinton machine though. And then there was race, and this was America, with its history of slavery, white supremacy, segregation, discrimination, lynching, the Ku Klux Klan, Bull Connor, George Wallace, violence, humiliation, murder and assassination. Perhaps, just perhaps though, that America only remained in embers, in footage of urban riots, protesters beaten by orgiastic police violence, and haunting images of violence against the individual, immortalised horror, disappearing but never to be forgotten.

Americans rose to the challenge. America is no longer a country that is defined by its racial fissures. Rather it is a country that is still seeking to contend with nearly two hundred years of legally sanctioned apartheid and even worse. There can be no greater testament to the progress that has been made than the basic fact that in the 2008 campaign, racial politics, though an ever-present, background factor, was only occasionally more than that. Even two decades ago it would have been a primary consideration and America would have split itself asunder. Instead, this election was about first and foremost its crunching economic travails but also concerned its place in the world, its future prospects, and its environmental challenges. Whenever race bubbled to the surface, it was dealt with in a calm and intelligent fashion. Twenty years previously, President George H. W. Bush was able to ride into the White House on the back of Lee Atwater's racially-charged campaign defined by the Willie Horton ad. That particular trough in the low art of presidential campaigning used the horrific story of a black criminal's heinous misdemeanours to mould race and crime together in a brutal attack on the Democratic candidate, Michael Dukakis.

No such stunt was pulled in 2008. Perhaps that is because it would not have worked or because things have moved on. That is progress. That is change.

So for the 80,000 people, in large part from Colorado itself, who had managed, through hustle, contacts, luck, commitment or personal importance, to get a ticket for this acceptance speech, there was an understanding that they were there not just to be applauding and cheering extras in a minor act of history. They were not there to see the latest romantic or quixotic attempt to prove that America is everything that they wanted to believe it to be. They were there to see this candidate elected, this dream come true, this hope fulfilled.

Then came the speech. Watched by another 38 million people across the nation, having hired a stadium, Barack Obama had to deliver. He did. The speech captured the essence of the moment, a country foundering abroad, suffering at home, with a politics seemingly unequal to the task, and a Federal Government that had turned in on itself and its institutions instead of focusing on the concerns of everyday middle and working-class America – Main Street in the vernacular.

By some strange contortion of fate, this very day 45 years previously, a young, oh so young, preacher, originally from Georgia, had addressed a crowd of his own. In front of the Lincoln Memorial in Washington, DC, Martin Luther King dared America to share his dream. Before somewhere between 200,000 and 250,000 people, Reverend King challenged America's politicians to let freedom ring. No more delay, no more steady as she goes. The time was now. With fierce urgency it was time to fulfil the promise etched into the Declaration of Independence itself. In King's irresistible plea: 'All men, yes, black men as well as white men, would be guaranteed the unalienable rights of life, liberty and the pursuit of happiness.'

He continued: 'And as we walk, we must make the pledge that we shall always march ahead. We cannot turn back.' Barack Obama matched the pace that Martin Luther King had set and declared, 'America, we cannot turn back, not with so much work to be done; not with so many children to educate, and veterans to care for; not with an economy to fix, cities to rebuild, and farms to save; not with so many families to protect and lives to mend. America we cannot turn back. We cannot walk alone. At this moment, in this election, we must pledge once more to march into the future.'

Thus began the renewal of the American dream. Barack Obama ended his acceptance speech echoing the spirit of that monumental Southern preacher. Martin Luther King and Barack Obama, through many twists and turns, are joined by more than an ethos. They are joined by history. It is the history of a movement for change.

❦

Movements have been an enduring feature of American politics over the last half-century. The success of Martin Luther King's Southern Christian Leadership Conference (SCLC) at the core of a broader civil rights movement exemplifies the potential power of the movement. By combining moral urgency with organisation, acute argument with mass participation, movements are able to induce, persuade and insist on change throughout politics, the legal system, education, commerce, and, in modern times, the media.

Movements sit outside and alongside political parties and campaigns, straddling culture and politics. They exist because democratic politics affords them an opportunity to influence. They are not formally part of the political system, however. They become attached to parties, to causes, to candidates, to caucuses, but they always retain their separateness. Indeed, that is part of their success. Sometimes movements seem to disappear, they become dormant, or shift shape, their values morphing into new causes for new times, attaching themselves to differing coalitions. When the historical camera is drawn backwards, however, suddenly the shapes become distinct, the agents identifiable, and the outcomes understood in the context of the movement's origins.

The civil rights movement is often seen as a relic of 1950s and 1960s America. Its promise and ultimate dream, at first the emancipation of African-Americans and then the greater cause of equality for all of America's dispossessed people, crumbled in 1968. Its leading light Martin Luther King was shot in Memphis. Its political hope was lost as Robert F. Kennedy was felled in the Ambassador Hotel in Los Angeles. It was finally defeated as police clubs, tear gas and water canon violently blinded and beat upon its believers outside the Chicago Convention in the summer of that year. Where hope had sprung eternal in the early part of the 1960s, exhaustion and fear had taken its place by the time that Richard Nixon was elected in the presidential election of 1968.

By then, a great deal had been achieved that would endure. Sometimes greatness steps onto your porch, rattles your shutter and demands to be let into your front room. In 1955, this happened to a preacher in Montgomery, Alabama, following the defiance by one of his townsfolk, Rosa Parks, who exhausted from a day's hard work as a seamstress, refused to make way when told to vacate her bus seat for the benefit of a white traveller. Martin Luther King answered the rap on the door and the Montgomery bus boycott was to be the beginning of a mission that would be defined by civil yet forceful protest.

King's movement was to 'March on Washington' following violent suppression of protest in Birmingham, Alabama. The march left the Lincoln Memorial that August day in 1963 to lobby the Kennedy administration to propose civil rights legislation that would sweep away slavery's deformed child, Jim Crow segregation. Separate can never be equal and when two races start from such an unequal footing, with the dominant of the two insistent on imposing its supremacy through law, economic control, state-sponsored violence and acceptance of non-state violence, i.e. lynching, there can be no hope for anything approaching justice.

If that was the central moral claim of the civil rights movement, its moral force was powered by the authority of nothing less than the founding document of the nation, the Declaration of Independence. The Declaration stated, explicitly: 'We hold these truths to be self-evident, that all men are created equal, that they are endowed by their creator with certain inalienable rights, that amongst these are life, liberty and the pursuit of happiness.' While the founding fathers may have been unwilling to confront the undeniable logic of their ethos, they had created the means by which first slavery and then Jim Crow would be demolished, and it took until 1964 for that to happen.

While the Kennedy administration conceded the point – it would seem that, as he whispered to King, he too had a dream – it took the navigational skills of Lyndon Johnson to turn that promise into reality. For someone who was to have such a decisive influence on the civil rights cause in America, Lyndon Johnson had kept his belief in racial justice and equality well hidden during his time in the US Senate. From opposing anti-lynching legislation to neutering the Civil Rights Act of 1957, Johnson was the very epitome of the segregationist conservative south. Just as greatness had come knocking for Martin Luther King, so it did for Lyndon Johnson – and he too answered the call. Following further atrocity at Selma's Edmund Pettus Bridge, where peaceful protesters were beaten following a voter registration campaign led by the Student Nonviolent Coordinating Committee (SNCC), President Johnson was galvanised.

In one of the great moments of political theatre, President Johnson declared to a joint session of Congress: 'What happened in Selma is part of a far larger movement which reaches into every section and the state of America. It is the effort of American Negroes to secure for themselves the full blessings of American life. Their cause must be our cause too because it is not just

Negroes, but really it is all of us, who must overcome this crippling legacy of bigotry and injustice.' He got it and then with a final dramatic flourish he exclaimed, 'And we shall overcome.'

Martin Luther King cried.* Within months, Johnson's Voting Rights Act was passed.

The civil rights movement now had a more solid foundation. From that point onwards African-Americans would have the vote and that would bring political influence to bear. Racial relations would, over time, change and voting rights were fundamental to that.

That historical achievement, fusing the mass energy of Martin Luther King with the guile and bravery of Lyndon Johnson, was the high-water mark of their relationship. Firstly, the Vietnam War would drive a wedge between them and then, as Martin Luther King broadened his movement to one representing all the dispossessed regardless of colour, creed, class or gender, he would contend with the multiple disappointments of an administration which, with an eye to the 1968 elections, would drift away from its liberal core.

Those two giants, Martin Luther King and Lyndon Johnson, might have created history in any decade. The incredible thing about the post-JFK 1960s was that there was a third figure who would sit alongside them both. Cruelly denied his opportunity to recast American politics, in his opposition to the Vietnam War and

---

*Robert A. Caro, *The Years of Lyndon Johnson: Means of Ascent*, p.xx.

in his obsessive desire to confront both rural and urban strains of deep poverty, Robert F. Kennedy would provide an emotional force to American politics that would be curtailed just as it looked like he was destined for the Democratic nomination in 1968. What Kennedy was beginning to achieve, briefly, was the drawing together of three movements: civil rights, peace and anti-poverty in a single movement for change.

It is to the thread left by Robert F. Kennedy that Barack Obama is reaching. When he entered the Senate in 2005, he was allocated the desk that had been occupied by Kennedy. His outsider status, his movement for change, his politics of equality and justice, his belief that through mobilisation America could fulfil its promise, his moral disgust at the neglect of America's black, urban ghettos, and his hands-on response, all echo Kennedy's urgent implorations for a better nation. Obama's insistence that *we can do better* was also the motivating energy of Kennedy's insurgency.

Different times mean different politics and there is a more moderate feel to Barack Obama's political creed. The underlying ethos though is the same and the means of securing change bears the silhouette of both Robert Kennedy's poetry of politics and his pragmatic mission. In *The Pursuit of Justice*, Kennedy wrote: 'Progress is a nice word. But change is its motivator. And change has its enemies. The willingness to confront change will determine how much we really do for our youth.'*

---

*Quoted in Jack Newfield, *RFK: A Memoir*, p. 72.

Perhaps in this quote more than any other, the golden thread, hidden in a time-worn tapestry that runs from Kennedy, stopping and winding around other people in other places, and finally to Obama, becomes visible. But by the middle of 1968 it seemed that the thread had been broken.

Johnson, Kennedy and King were bound and entangled with one another, each achievement shared, each animosity mutually felt. As it is with all movements, no individual can claim the greater achievement than the other. Was it King's ability to inspire a mass movement? Johnson's ability to get laws passed? Or Kennedy's continuous moral voice? Between the imagined and the secured, there is a world of possibility.

When these titans left the political stage, so went the possibility of a movement for justice that stretched further, burrowed deeper, and achieved more of its aims. As it happened the social and political chaos of 1968 as well as the gathering economic storms created an opening for the first President at the head of a reactionary movement.

Richard M. Nixon demonstrated the political possibility of a right-leaning movement based on traditional values, economic conservatism, and national prestige and power. In the undergrowth, the most formidable election-winning machine was being assembled. It was based around a mass movement of social, economic and neo-conservatives, of ideas infused with moral and religious disgust, of nationalism meeting mass mobilisation, and self-interest cross-cutting corporate influence.

In many senses, the history of post-1960s America is one of two great movements. One, the movement for justice, was vanquished when, denied its leadership, it over-stretched itself. The other, the conservative movement, secured presidential office for twenty-eight of the next forty years, in the process spawning its own political, socio-economic class, the 'Reagan Democrats.' Only presidential crookedness through Watergate which gave Jimmy Carter his victory in 1976 and economic recession highlighted and dissembled by one of the great political communicators, Bill Clinton, in 1992, would deny the conservative movement an even greater period of office.

Despite the success of the conservative movement, the liberal movement did not die. It fragmented, it dispersed, but crucially it remained alive. Its most powerful and active arm was to be found in a city to which Martin Luther King had devoted his attention in the latter years of his life. Those very same civil rights activists who persuaded him to move north now fused with a powerful independent politics that would be the prototype and test-bed for the movement politics that would determine Barack Obama's success. Chicago, its neighbourhoods and its politics, is a central part of the Barack Obama story.

Barack Obama arrived in Chicago in 1985, moving there from New York to become a community organiser in the deprived neighbourhoods of Roseland and Calumet. A callow youth with an idealistic outlook and a native gift for people and prose; a young man with a mission, this youthful Barack Obama was bursting with desire for change, a lonely traveller with a incomplete map and a hazy destination.

His first observation of Chicagoan politics was an inspirational one. Chicago had elected its first black Mayor in 1983. The golden thread, seemingly broken in 1968, had been kept intact in Chicago by Jesse Jackson Sr amongst others. Through the civil rights movement, African-Americans had been given the promise of not just civil rights but also political power. In Chicago, a group of enlightened politicians and political activists had determined, once the possibility presented itself with the death of Mayor Richard J. Daley after more than two decades of iron grip on the city, to make that promise a reality. The chosen tools were voter registration and reaching out to other communities.

Initially, these activists, representing a powerful minority that still was not powerful enough to gain control of City Hall, had backed Jane Byrne for Mayor in 1979. Byrne had promised to redistribute resources and political power away from downtown business and into the neglected neighbourhoods. She reneged on her promises and quickly became a willing political hostage of what remained of the Daley machine. Chicago's black community never forgave her and set about removing her from office in 1983. When her vote in the Democratic primary was split by the entrance into the race of Richard J. Daley's son, Richard M. Daley, the possibility for an historic victory was set.

A coalition of the African-American community, a

portion of the Latino community, 'Hyde Park' liberals and the student vote came in behind Harold Washington, an inspirational and independently-minded black politician who defeated Byrne for the Democratic nomination. It was the political activism born out of the civil rights ethos that created the possibility. Washington won the mayoral election, just, and with stiff opposition, set about opening up Chicago's politics and redirecting energy and resources to the neighbourhoods. When Barack Obama had applied for a job in Washington's office he got no response. So it was to the South Side in Chicago that he turned.

In his early memoirs he recounts his experiences in one particular neighbourhood that left a lasting impression on him, Altgeld Gardens.

It is easy to imagine Altgeld Gardens as a more thriving community than it is today. In fact, in the 1950s and 1960s it was. More a staging post for upwardly-mobile black families on their way to owning their own family homes, increasingly it became an isolated island of welfare dependence and deprivation. Bounded by Chicago's South Side steel mills that were the economic life support machine of the community, its gradual decline became despair when that support was cut off. Like a nation with a dependence on a single crop that is devastated after a poor harvest, the closure of the steel mills, industrial decline homing in on the community, left the neighbourhood bereft.

Today, Altgeld Gardens has its committed community activists, its families led mainly by mothers desperate to make the most of trying circumstances, and its collective humour. Bright lights shine from a fog of unemployment, gangs, drugs, mental health concerns, welfare dependence, family breakdown, persistent crime from the petty to deadly serious, educational underperformance and the denial of access to culture and hope.

To write off an entire community is to write off the hope of individuals. Still people strive to prevent this community from sinking altogether. People like Paulette Edwards, a family support worker (who has devoted her life to just ensuring that even a handful of kids get the chances they deserve), desperately and intelligently seek to engineer hope. The voices of Altgeld Gardens resonate. They should haunt because there must be a moral urgency to prevent whole communities from going under.

Barack Obama's legacy endures in Altgeld Gardens: he transformed the lives of many who came into contact with him. The neighbourhood left an even greater impression on him. The plight of Altgeld Gardens is by no means unique in modern America and adds an even greater urgency to the need for change.

By the time of Barack Obama's arrival in Chicago, some remarkable people had already worked to achieve change in Chicago. The election of Harold Washington in 1983 and, again, in 1987 was the achievement of a group of people who were masters of the technique of politics. Many were refugees from the civil rights movement and this political endeavour is the umbilical link between

Martin Luther King and Barack Obama. Their mission was to drag the attention of Chicago's politics towards neighbourhoods such as Altgeld Gardens, the urban blight that was a consequence of Chicago's *de facto* and politically manipulated segregation. Equally interesting is the fact that the techniques, strategies, and, indeed, some of the personnel involved in that moment of change, the election of Chicago's first black mayor, were passed onto Barack Obama a decade and a half or so later.

Barack Obama's presidential campaign was a projection of the movement for justice that floundered but never died following 1968. Its transmission through Chicago's independent political forces is a critical element to understanding Barack Obama's transition from idealistic organiser to presidential candidate. It would seem that, far from dying in 1968, this movement simply dispersed and lay low in Chicago and elsewhere for a while before roaring back to life in the 1980s. Then, infused by the political personality and leadership of Barack Obama, it adopted a new mission, the election of America's first black President.

The movement for change comes to the fore just as the conservative movement, creaking under the weight of its internal contradictions, seems to be facing its most challenging period since its inception. The mobilising force of the movement kept the presidency in Republican hands by the narrowest of margins in 2000 and 2004 but that energy and sense of collective mission has weakened and has faced its greatest defeats in 2006 and now 2008.

With his army of volunteers and voters, his organisation, his personality and his leadership, Barack Obama has the first opportunity for two generations to translate fleeting electoral success into an enduring movement for change. At every stage of his remarkable political career he has written fresh and exciting chapters into American political folklore. In defeating the Clinton machine, coming from nowhere to win the White House, the heady pace of his political rise, and the organisation and campaign that he has created, Barack Obama has placed himself at the centre of America's political landscape.

His opportunity now is to do something that his political forebears failed to achieve. That is to create a generation of change: one that rebuilds America's reputation abroad, confronts its environmental morass, creates an economy and society that spreads wealth and opportunity rather than hoards it at the top, and fashions a political culture that is engaged with its people and gives them the power to initiate change. These are goals that go beyond the presidency. America has the realisable opportunity to once again fulfil its elemental promise. For that, a movement for change that reaches across generations and cultures and endures beyond an electoral cycle or two is needed.

Barack Obama has an historic opportunity to lead such a movement. His greatest achievement could be to create something that can reach beyond his presidency, into towns, neighbourhoods and communities and to the next generation, and the next, and beyond that also.

Change would become not merely embedded in laws but would be embraced in the souls and actions of people and would thus have much greater resilience.

'Politics is the art of the possible,' as Otto von Bismarck once said. Now, in 2009, in America, as happens from time to time, politics is the art of everything possible.

Race, Poverty and Ho Chi Minh

BARACK OBAMA IS FOND of quoting Martin Luther King's optimistic vision: 'The arc of the moral universe is long but it bends towards justice.' It was in the 1950s that that arc began its journey through time, politics, law and society, turning America onto the path of the promise intrinsic to the Declaration of Independence.

In overturning *Plessy v Ferguson*, an 1896 Supreme Court ruling that had upheld the notion that separate could mean equal, the era of civil rights began. *Brown v Board of Education, Topeka* was more than the end of legal segregation of public schools. It was hope. Post-Civil War America's tolerance of legal, economic and social segregation could come to an end. With the strong arm of a brilliant generation of men, from civil rights leaders to Supreme Court Justices to Presidents to right-minded people willing to add their voice to the moral outrage, the arc bent towards justice.

What began in 1954 ended in political exhaustion in

1968. As peace protestors were brutalised in Chicago, the movement for change collapsed in the face of a conservative counter-revolution began with the election of Richard Nixon in November of that year.

Segregated America was a country where a young boy called Emmett Till was lynched, cruelly beaten, tortured, murdered, his body cast into the Tallahatchie River, Mississippi, for no crime greater than getting a little fresh with a store clerk. It was a society where Governors of southern states used their power to block integration of state educational facilities. A myriad of department stores, buses, public washrooms, canteens, doctor's surgeries, schools, were segregated on grounds of race. That America, its Apartheid lingering even now as a historical stench, is only a couple of generations or so away. The inheritance and successes of the 1960s civil rights movement extends to today's politicians, Barack Obama included.

Amongst the many achievements, it was perhaps voting rights that were the most critical. A voice at the political table, ultimately, is what agitates for change.

Early in his involvement in the civil rights movement, Martin Luther King himself had seen this imperative: 'The chief weapon in our fight for civil rights is the vote. Do you realise what would happen … if three million voters were added to the rolls in the South?'* When the Voting Rights Act was passed in 1965, there were only 100 African-Americans who held elective office, all in the North, but by 1989 there were more than 7,200. In

---

*Marshall Frady, *Martin Luther King, Jr: A Life*, p. 153.

fact, one of Martin Luther King's lieutenants, Andrew Young, became Mayor of Atlanta, and John Lewis, the quietly spoken but inspirational leader who had such a central role in the removal of barriers to voter registration, and was knocked unconscious at Selma for his troubles, became Congressman for Georgia's 5th congressional district.

Voting rights were achieved but the movement was left leaderless and moving to the fringe of popular acceptability by 1968. In the face of violence, riots, ever more extreme voices in and splitting from its ranks, a cowering white America faced 'Black Power' with trepidation and was afraid.

As it happens the movement left a thread for posterity. That thread would become clearer to the older Barack Obama once he became actively engaged in Chicago in the 1980s, politically from the 1990s onwards. Just as countless others would, not just in politics but in all walks of life, the young Barack Obama, born on August 4, 1961 and brought up in Hawaii and Indonesia, would feel the inspirational force of the 1960s more immediately because it struck at his very essence: his unresolved identity and search for true belonging. Indeed, his employer at the Developing Communities Project in Chicago's South Side, Jerry Kellman said: 'Barack had been very inspired by the civil rights movement. I felt that he wanted to work in the civil rights movement but he was ten years too late.'* Ten years late he may have

---

*National Review, June 30, 2008.

been but the movement had still infused his character and his political DNA.

❧

In the preface to the 2004 edition of *Dreams from My Father*, Barack Obama explains the original motivation for writing such a precocious book at the age of thirty-three: 'I received an advance from a publisher and went to work with the belief that the story of my family, and my efforts to understand that story, might speak in some way to the fissures of race that have characterised the American experience, as well as the fluid state of identity – the leaps through time, the collision of cultures – that mark our modern life.'*

His search for this understanding, perhaps inspired by an absent and then deceased father, was sparked and nurtured by his mother, Ann Dunham. The preface is concluded, slightly ruefully following his mother's death, with the reflection: 'I think sometimes that had I known she would not survive her illness, I might have written a different book – less a meditation on the absent parent, more a celebration of the one who was the single constant in my life.'†

It is not surprising that a young man with a Kenyan father and Kansan mother is faced with both a constant search for his own identity and confusion at a world

---

*Barack Obama, *Dreams from My Father*, 2004 edition, p. vii.
†*Dreams from My Father*, p. xii.

that just doesn't seem to place him in the same way that he places himself. What is fascinating about the story is the part that America's strained race relations had to play on his mother's life as well as the life of her family. In fact, though he does not explicitly state it, there is a hint that a particular incident back when the family were living in Kansas had an impact on her father's decision to move the family to Hawaii.

One day, Ann Dunham's mother, Madelyn Dunham came home to find a confrontation between her daughter and some of the kids from the neighbourhood in progress. The kids were shouting racial obscenities at her daughter and, at one point, a stone was even thrown. Ann had been sharing her books with a black girl from the neighbourhood and when this gang discovered that, they decided to let their bullying displeasure be known. Ann and her friend were clearly upset and Ann's father, Stanley Dunham, 'Gramps', was furious. He called the parents of all the children involved to register his disgust at their children's behaviour but was met with the same attitude from each one, 'You best talk to your daughter, Mr Dunham. White girls don't play with the coloureds in this town.'*

His grandfather would insist that they had left Texas because of the racism and that this incident in Kansas distressed him deeply and left a rupture in his affection with Kansas. There was a deep desire within the Dunham family to live in a different type of America, whose

_____
*Dreams from My Father, p. 20.

image they felt could be glimpsed, to some extent, in the Hawaii of the 1960s.

Even there, however, casual and visceral racism had an uncomfortable prevalence. Gramps upbraids a passer-by for his throwaway comment, on seeing his grandson swimming in the ocean, on how well 'they' could swim. He can't help showing his disgust with 'Toot', Barack's grandmother, who having been accosted by a panhandler on the bus journey the previous day, then tries to get a lift to work. He is furious and Barack seems to be confused about his anger. Surely it's no big deal? Gramps replies, 'It *is* a big deal. It's a big deal to me. She's been bothered by men before. You know why she's so scared this time? I'll tell you why. Before you came in, she told me the fella was *black*. That's the real reason why she's bothered. And I just don't think that's right.' For his grandson, the words were like 'a fist in my stomach.'* This was but a single incident. Toot, who tragically died on the eve of the election – but not before she had cast her absentee ballot – was the rock and foundation of the family and Barack Obama owed her his enormous devotion and gratitude.

Something of Obama's grandfather's searing sense of justice and equality seem to have passed from father to daughter. Her mother, Madelyn, described Ann Dunham as an 'Adlai Stevenson liberal.'† That seems to understate her politics which was far more proactive,

---

* *Dreams from My Father,* p. 88.
† David Mendell, *Barack Obama: From Promise to Power,* p. 24.

more hands-on, and less aloof and intellectual than that of the two-time Democratic presidential candidate, Adlai Stevenson. She was no Ivy League bien-pensant liberal. She lived her convictions through actions rather than words much as her son was later to do in Chicago's South Side. She went about this by working for the Ford Foundation on women's issues in Jakarta and her involvement on micro-finance projects in Pakistan and Indonesia.*

Barack Obama's father left Ann when he was just two years old. Ann took Barack to Indonesia with her to live with her second husband Lolo, along with a pet monkey (or *ape* as Ann would correct Barack). In those Indonesian years, Ann would also become Barack's teacher, not only in basic reading and arithmetic at eye-stingingly early hours of the morning, but on his cultural heritage also.

She would return home clutching books on the civil rights movement, the recordings of Mahalia Jackson and the speeches of Dr King. Obama writes: 'If I told her about the goose-stepping demonstrations of my Indonesian Boy Scout troop performed in front of the President, she might mention a different kind of march, a march of children no older than me, a march for freedom. Every black man was Thurgood Marshall or Sidney Poitier; every black woman Fannie Lou Hamer or Lena Horne. To be black was to be the beneficiary of a great inheritance, a special destiny, glorious burdens

---

The New York Times, March 14, 2008.

that only we were strong enough to bear. Burdens we were to carry in style. More than once, my mother would point out: "Harry Belafonte is the best–looking man on the planet."*

In those conversations, the shared moments of a mother and son, Barack would receive more than cultural reassurance. He would have the psychological preparation for imagined and probable racial slights further down the road. He and countless others like him came to understand that they could overcome. With spirit, and verve, and words, and solidarity, and courage, and relentlessness, they too could bend that arc. That self-belief, not in destiny, but in the force of change, was a gift given to all subsequent generations by a remarkable leader: Martin Luther King.

❧

It is difficult to imagine three men with a greater gulf in disposition than Martin Luther King, Lyndon Baines Johnson and Robert Francis Kennedy. The sum of their achievements was considerable. But two would be assassinated; one would leave office broken-hearted. When the scene of the wreckage was surveyed, enormous advances had been made, but their cause had overheated. Accelerating ever faster, it was just impossible to keep everyone on board and the vehicle left the road.

---

*Dreams from My Father, pp. 50–51.

There was little in Lyndon Johnson's early biography that would hint at greatness to come. He had neither the rhetorical flair of a Martin Luther King nor the sense of entitlement that was Bobby Kennedy's inheritance. Born in poverty, dipping in and out of penury in Texas, brilliant in private, generous of nature, fragile but incomparably determined, Johnson was a force of nature, a whirlwind of political energy which when properly directed was irresistible. This Texan hustler had accumulated power out of nothing, building the type of congressional power base that even his mentors Senator Richard Russell of Georgia and Congressman Sam Rayburn were unable to amass.

What virtue is power without purpose? might be the political epitaph of his years as the most powerful majority leader of the Senate yet seen. For, in 1960, his final year in the post prior to assuming the vice-presidency, it was not at all clear that this 'Master of the Senate' as his biographer Robert A. Caro describes him, was destined for anything other than achieving mastery over the technique of power.

Neither would it have been clear that, as Johnson was later to share with his official biographer, Doris Kearns Goodwin, he wanted power to 'give things to people – all sorts of people, especially the poor and the blacks.'*

After all, this was the same Lyndon Johnson who as Senate Majority Leader had emasculated the 1957 Civil

---

*Doris Kearns Goodwin, *Lyndon Johnson and the American Dream*, p. 54.

Rights Act rendering it meaningless. As Senator Wayne Morse was to say on the floor of the Senate: 'I disagree with my majority leader on the nature of the bill. I consider it a corpse. I think this so-called Civil Rights Bill shows that civil rights for the time being for millions of coloured people are dead, so far as effective protection of their right to vote is concerned.'* Craftily, Johnson had manoeuvred a key provision out of the legislation that would have allowed federal government agents to protect civil rights. He also inserted a provision that all civil rights cases should be tried before a jury. *To Kill a Mockingbird* juries meant no genuine extension of civil rights. This along with the absence of federal enforcement meant that the bill was more gum than teeth.

Had Martin Luther King been observing the Senate machinations in any detail, the notion that this gigantic and all-powerful senator would be the President who would not only enable passage of the most comprehensive civil rights measures since Lincoln's Emancipation Proclamation but would also pass effective voting rights legislation, would have been peculiar.

Equally, on entering the Oval Office in 1963, that Johnson would be, 'the President who finishes what Lincoln began,'† would have likely attracted deep Southern mirth. That is precisely what Lyndon Johnson did achieve. Though given a shove by Martin Luther King, and shamed by the brutal suppression of the peaceful

---

Johnson and the American Dream, p. 152.
†Stephen Graubard, *The Presidents*, p. 451.

march in Selma, when he arrived at the realisation that it was his destiny to act, he seized the opportunity. In so doing, he became what he always wanted to be: a hero. At least he did for a while.

None of this is to diminish in the slightest the contribution made by Martin Luther King to the cause nor President John F. Kennedy who first introduced the civil rights legislation to Congress. It is just that President Johnson's skill in not just navigating Congress, which he better knew than anyone, but also in inspiring Congress to face the reality of the unjust social divides in the nation, were game changers in achieving workable civil rights legislation. He used the memory of a slain President to shame Congress into passing the Civil Rights Act in 1964 and he gave the speech of his life to a joint session of Congress to demand that a Voting Rights Act became law in 1965 following the violence at Selma.

After declaring to an electrified Congress that 'We shall overcome', he grabbed the lapels of the Chairman of the Judiciary Committee, Congressman Emanuel Celler and said: 'Manny, I want you to start hearings tonight.' Celler said that it couldn't be done before the following week. Johnson replied: 'Start them *this* week, Manny. And hold night sessions too.'* That is exactly what happened and so a bill that had been sent to Congress on March 17, 1965 was signed by the President on August 6th of the same year. Through determination,

---

*Robert A. Caro, *The Years of Lyndon Johnson: Means of Ascent*, p. xxi.

insider knowledge, and the force of his political personality President Johnson had secured his great contribution to American history.

President Johnson's achievements on the domestic front were remarkable. Not all proved as durable as the civil rights legislation but in his attempt to wrap the nation in the warm blanket of public provision, he was nothing if not generous. The public health provisions for elderly and deprived families, Medicare and Medicaid, were initiated as part of Johnson's 'Great Society' mission that constituted a federally mandated 'War on Poverty.' Head Start, designed to help disadvantaged preschool children, was also initiated at this time. Vocational training was expanded, welfare payouts were increased, immigration was made less discriminatory and the Department of Housing and Urban Development was established to combine housing provision with the types of intervention that would improve the employment prospects and life chances of its inhabitants. In almost every imaginable way President Johnson sought to use the strength of Federal intervention to improve people's lives.

Many of the measures failed to be sure. In economic terms, it was ambitious to implement these measures whilst committing to a very expensive war in South East Asia. Towards the end of his tenure, as inflation was rising, Johnson was forced to go to Congress to ask for a tax rise. More was being asked of the taxpayer and there was increasing concern that the only beneficiaries of this largesse were minority or fringe groups.

That is not to criticise the ambition or even the achievement of Lyndon Johnson's Presidency. On the domestic front, he would perhaps be talked of in the same terms as his hero Franklin Delano Roosevelt, had it not been for the knock-on effect of a costly and failed war in a far-off land. Johnson paid the ultimate price for escalating the US involvement in Vietnam. Not only would he be forced into retirement but his reputation would forever be tarnished. It was this brutal, humiliating and failed attempt to stem the communist contagion that would shred his reputation and bring him into direct conflict with not only Martin Luther King but Robert F. Kennedy as well.

'Hey, hey, LBJ, how many kids did you kill today?' That was the chant that reverberated off the walls of the White House night after night as the Vietnam War escalated, starting off as a peace-keeping mission and ending in the horror of a bloody and pointless war seemingly without end. It would get louder and louder and louder until it implanted itself into the consciousness of the President himself. Johnson and Martin Luther King had been spiritual brothers-in-arms but now they were headed on a collision course. Vietnam was the guillotine blade that detached Lyndon Baines Johnson from the civil rights movement.

When King had met President Johnson for the first time, he had been charmed, as so many were. On assuming the Presidency, Johnson had summoned him and other civil rights leaders to the White House and assured them that John F. Kennedy's civil rights legislation would be passed 'without a word or comma changed.'* His character and commitment would convince Dr King that he had an ally in the White House. The sense of mutual purpose and personal understanding would collapse.

President Johnson's drift away from the 'Great Society' mission and the 'War on Poverty' was certainly part of the reason for the separation. Not least, President Johnson had responded with a law and order mentality to the riots in 1967 in Detroit and Newark, ignoring the Kerner Commission Report that had looked at the underlying causes of those riots and came to the conclusion that $30 billion need to be invested in combating urban poverty. The figure was similar to that which Martin Luther King had been touting around as part of his Poor People's Campaign.†

But, as King had articulated it in a speech in Los Angeles in February 1967: 'Despite feeble protestations to the contrary, the promises of the Great Society have been shot down on the battlefield of Vietnam.'

At the same time an old friend was emerging as a new ally. Though King would never endorse this ally directly, as they both had too much to lose for this to be sensible, they had more in common politically. This new ally wholeheartedly believed in the onward march of justice and equality but was against the bloody

---

*Marshall Frady, *Martin Luther King, Jr: A Life*, p. 133.
†Rick Perlstein, *Nixonland: The Rise of a President and the Fracturing of America*, p. 239.

quagmire of the Vietnam War. That candidate was Robert F. Kennedy and his campaign and persona were very different to any that had gone before.

❧

Robert F. Kennedy was an ultra-establishment figure who shed that chrysalis to metamorphose into the ultimate people's movement politician. The civil rights movement had found Martin Luther King. Now, the gathering new politics of peace, civil rights, and anti-poverty, manifested in citizen action, in marches, petitions, citizen journalism and political action, found Kennedy.

Given that the Democratic candidate in 1972, George McGovern, was able to command similar forces, but was crushed by President Nixon by 520 to 17 electoral votes, and given that extensive civil rights legislation and its social impact would produce a reaction that would give Republicans an opportunity to win the South, it would be a brave counter-factual to suggest that this new movement would have secured the presidency for Robert F. Kennedy in 1968. But then, George McGovern was no Robert F. Kennedy.

The Kennedy that emerged in the aftermath of his brother's death was thoughtful, erudite, moral, visionary, angry but astute, the charismatic orator who served as a lightning conductor for the deep liberal concern at the path the nation was taking. President Johnson loathed him. He also feared him.

Kearns Goodwin writes: 'Johnson had desperately tried to keep alive the distinction between the doer and the thinker ... Yet here was a man who seemed to combine both intellect and will.'* Perhaps the origin of this antipathy was in Robert Kennedy's shuttle diplomacy with Lyndon Johnson at the Democratic Convention of 1960 when despite being offered the vice-presidency, Johnson felt that he had been treated with disdain by Kennedy. Perhaps it was the proximity to the new President that Robert enjoyed as Attorney General in John F. Kennedy's administration. Lyndon Johnson felt isolated and impotent and this was tough on someone who had ruled the Senate. Perhaps there was a basic personality difference that could never be reconciled.

Had Bobby Kennedy been a liberal dreamer then Johnson could have simply dismissed him as an elite intellectual without the practical knowledge of life and politics necessary to make a real difference. Kennedy though was a combination of intellectual and practitioner which made him difficult to place and impossible to dismiss.

The aura of the Kennedy presidency surrounded him. But he was not a throwback, a sentimental repeat performance of an already bygone age. By 1968, he was not only a formidable politician in his own right but a direct and potentially fatal threat to Johnson's chances of re-nomination for the Democratic ticket. The personal and the political were colliding spectacularly

---

*Doris Kearns Goodwin, p. 201.

just as Johnson's presidency was beginning to crumble through failures abroad and increasing economic turmoil at home. More than a perfect storm, this was a hurricane of unimaginable force.

Robert F. Kennedy's early career had included a period of service as Assistant Counsel to Senator Joseph McCarthy's Senate Permanent Subcommittee on Investigations. He then went on to be Chief Counsel to the Senate Labor Rackets Committee which brought him into direct confrontation with Jimmy Hoffa, boss of the Teamsters Union. He then went on to serve as the second youngest Attorney General ever under John F. Kennedy. This early biography hardly reads as that of a man who was to bring together a popular movement aimed at securing the presidency, ending a failing war, and launching a new crusade to eliminate poverty and suffering.

By the time that he announced he was running for the presidency in March 1968, he had in mind an insurgent campaign that would take on his party's elite and win. His aide Adam Walinsky made this clear: 'Our strategy is to change the rules of nominating a President. We're going to do it a new way. In the street.'* Kennedy himself would make clear the type of coalition he had in mind. He would confide in his friend, former advisor and ally, Jack Newfield: 'We have to convince the Negroes and poor whites that they have common interests. If we can reconcile those two hostile groups,

---

*Jack Newfield, *RFK: A Memoir*, p. 230.

and then add the kids, you can really turn this country around."*

It was this coalition, a movement based around civil rights, the war and anti-poverty, which carried him to spectacular victories in Nebraska, Indiana, and, most crucially in terms of his ability to secure the Democratic nomination, California. It was during the celebrations following the California victory that he was assassinated in the Ambassador Hotel in Los Angeles.

❧

The loosening of Robert F. Kennedy's partisan allegiance to the Johnson presidency happened for two reasons: Johnson's response to the challenges posed by urban poverty and his conduct of the Vietnam War. Race and poverty would collide explosively throughout the 1960s. For anyone whose analysis of race deprivation was based on legal barriers to equality alone, the 1960s would shake them from their slumber. Poverty demanded immediate attention and resolution. Ultimately, America would weary of the fight, closing its eyes to a problem seemingly so intractable that it was felt little could be achieved.

As early as 1955, Martin Luther King had sought to reach beyond a narrow racial conception of the plight of modern America. Montgomery was just part of a wider struggle for Dr King. That struggle was not

---

*Jack Newlfield, p. 253.

simply racial in character. It was about class too. He declared: 'The Negro cannot be free as long as there are poor and underprivileged white people. Equality for Negroes is related to the greater problem of economic uplift for Negroes and the poor white man.'* Eventually, this embracing philosophy would define Dr King and would culminate in the fiercely ambitious Poor People's Campaign which aimed not just to dissolve class barriers and eradicate inequality, but also to eliminate poverty.

At the beginning of the 1960s, there was one America: prosperous, consumerist, secure, upwardly mobile, suburban, white, empowered, educated, and yet more insecure and fearful than it dared to admit. But there was another America too. It was this America that drew the piercing and empathetic gaze of the writer Michael Harrington, in his devastating critique of modern American society and its 40–50 million economic and social orphans. This 'other America', the 'invisible land', consisted of tens of millions who were, 'at this very moment, maimed in body and spirit, existing at levels beneath those necessary for human decency. If these people are not starving, they are hungry, and sometimes fat with hunger, for that is what cheap foods do. They are without adequate housing and education and medical care.'†

What was worse was the invisibility of the poor.

---

*Marshall Frady, p. 53.
†Michael Harrington, p. 9.

Harrington wrote: 'Here is a great mass of people, yet it takes an effort of the intellect and will even to see them.'* America had the best-dressed poverty in the world, the sartorial adornments of mass production having been spread widely. Yet this mass of people were too old to be seen, they were politically invisible as they were not members of unions or parties and, of course, in the case of Southern African-Americans in particular, were not even registered to vote. 'That the poor are invisible is one of the most important things about them. They are not simply neglected and forgotten as in the old rhetoric of reform; what is much worse, they are not seen,' Harrington concluded.†

A technological revolution was hitting America, one in which the means of production were shifting to more highly skilled manufacturing and service industries. The highly educated, skilled or professional classes had everything to gain and the lesser skilled classes had everything to lose. This economic change, mitigated to a greater or lesser extent during the Johnson years, has continued apace right up to the present day.

Between 1953 and 1959, 1.5 million blue-collar jobs, 11 percent of the total, were eliminated from the economy, and at the same time the number of clerical and professional workers increased by 600,000.‡ A crude economic analysis would predict an over-supply of

---

*Michael Harrington, p. 12.
†Michael Harrington, p. 14.
‡Michael Harrington, p. 36.

workers at the bottom end of the economy. Statistics and economic analysis are fine, but these were real people such as the African-American workers whom Harrington met in Chicago.

They had worked in the meat-packing industry and were members of the Packinghouse Workers Unions (unions were the one bulwark against misery, that is if you could find work and be accepted as a member). They had been earning $2.25 an hour, which was a relatively sound wage for a worker in the early 1960s, and they had benefits such as sick leave, vacation pay and, more importantly, a personal dignity and the respect of their family. When they lost their jobs at the Armour meat-packing firm, some of them found non-unionised, seasonal work at a Christmas tree manufacturing factory making only $1 an hour.* These workers constituted a reserve army of cheap labour that could bid down all wages at the bottom end of the income scale. It is no wonder that in these conditions racial suspicion was rife.

The Christmas tree worker thus faced the 'double indignity' of racial discrimination and economic oppression. However, important as legislative reform was for the former, it would not be sufficient. As Harrington put it: 'If all the discrimination laws in the United States were immediately repealed, race would still remain as one of the most pressing moral and political states.'†

Harrington was an exceedingly influential voice on

---

*Michael Harrington, pp. 30–32.
†Michael Harrington, p. 72.

the left in the 1960s, his work having both a powerful impact on John F. Kennedy and serving as the catalyst for the 'War on Poverty' under President Johnson. In warning that civil rights legislation wasn't enough, he was prescient. Following the signing of the Civil Rights Act 1964, riots broke out in Harlem, New York.

Then riots broke out again after the passage of the Voting Rights Act the next year, this time in the Watts neighbourhood of Los Angeles. These were even more serious than the riots in Harlem. 34 people were killed, over 1,000 injured and over 3,000 arrested. What on earth was going on? President Johnson was certainly bemused. He pleaded, 'How is it possible after all we've accomplished? How could it be? Is the world topsy-turvy?'*

If he had re-read his Michael Harrington he would understand precisely why. At the very point that legislators and the courts had started to respond to the legal inequality facing African-Americans, there was a realisation that new concessions could and should be won. The Harlem and Watts riots were only the beginning. More and worse was to come.

In 1966, four African-Americans were killed in six days of rioting in Cleveland, Ohio. Similar confrontations took place in Chicago and San Francisco. Then came the even more serious riots of 1967. 26 people died in Newark and hundreds were injured after six days of rioting was sparked off by the arrest and beating

---

*Doris Kearns Goodwin, p. 305.

of a local cab driver. In Detroit in the same year, a riot ensued after a police raid on an unlicensed bar. 43 people died, 467 were injured, 7,200 people were arrested and 2,000 buildings were burned down.

Every year, the riots seemed to be happening with greater regularity and intensity. The impact on race relations was irretrievably harmful. In 1964, 34 percent of Americans believed that African-Americans were trying to 'move too fast.' By 1966 that percentage had increased to 85 percent.*

President Johnson was determined to get to the bottom of what was happening. On July 29, 1967, he signed an Order to establish the National Advisory Commission on Civil Disorders. The Commission, which would acquire the name of its chairman, Governor Kerner of Illinois, was asked three basic questions: *What happened? Why did it happen? What can be done to prevent it from happening again and again?* Johnson would not like the answer at all.

The famous conclusion of the report was scathing: 'Our nation is moving toward two societies, one black, one white – separate and unequal.' Its content was just as uncompromising. White society was 'deeply' implicated in the ghetto: 'White institutions created it, white institutions maintain it, and white society condones it.' So the ghetto was not just a voluntary concentration of ethnicity, it had been created through economic structures (including the housing market), public

---

*Doris Kearns Goodwin, p. 304.

agencies and differential economic opportunity, and it was fiercely oppressed and suppressed by the strong arm of the law.

The solution that the Kerner Commission proposed was all-encompassing: 'It is time to make good the promises of American democracy to all citizens – urban and rural, white and black, Spanish-surname, American-Indian, and every minority.' What the Commission had in mind was an all-guns-blazing attack on the scourge of American racism and poverty. While President Johnson had been inclined to see the riots as a breakdown of law and order, Kerner was more inclined to the view of those who had been involved. It was rebellion rather than rioting and, if anything, there was an inevitability to it given the embedded and concentrated deprivation that lay at its heart.

President Johnson ignored the report. He refused to even receive a copy. Quite what he had expected the Commission to come up with is not clear. In all probability, it was something less comprehensive. Almost certainly, he would have expected some amount of blame to go to what he considered were lawless rioters. The frontline of American civil and now social rights had moved from the South to the mainly northern metropolises. It was a shift that led to a change in strategy for Martin Luther King.

In 1966, Dr King was persuaded by Jesse Jackson to move his campaign north to Chicago. The challenge was perhaps even greater than he faced in the South. Racial discrimination was far more covert in Chicago than the overt racism of the South. It manifested itself in slum housing, *de facto* segregation and denial of economic opportunity. Its demoralising effect was no less severe but it was much more difficult to isolate and eliminate. In Mayor Richard J. Daley he found far too wily an opponent. He was more than willing to agree to all of King's demands but he never committed to a timetable for implementation. *De facto* segregation in Chicago was far less amenable to political negotiation and reform through statute.

Chicago was a city with a tightly-woven tradition of racial discrimination that would take long painstaking effort to change. Though Dr King achieved very little in Chicago he did leave a legacy. Jesse Jackson remained and from there he would take the civil rights movement down a political road, one that would eventually join forces with those behind the Harold Washington for Mayor campaign. That critical victory of 1983 would create an organisation, a political base, and a set of tactics that, ultimately, would transfer to Barack Obama in the first part of the twenty-first century.

�֍

Martin Luther King's concerns were also those of Robert F. Kennedy. The plight of the modern American ghettoised city had led Kennedy, as a New York Senator, to take an intellectual and practical interest in the (largely) mono-ethnic urban prison of Bedford-Stuyvesant. Again, the statistics tend to shield the real-life stories of desperation and inspiration that exist in a place such as Bedford-Stuyvesant. They are worth repeating nonetheless. In the Bedford-Stuyvesant of the mid-1960s, 36 percent of families were headed by women, 80 percent of teenagers were high school dropouts. It had the highest infant mortality rate and more than 90 percent of the housing was built before 1920 with almost half of it classified as 'dilapidated and insufficient.'* Bedford-Stuyvesant was where poor black families (and some Puerto Rican families) went to live if they couldn't make ends meet in Harlem.

Kennedy decided that he was going to personally find a way of initiating change and uplifting this desperate ghetto. The private sector would be encouraged to invest through tax incentives and the area would be uplifted physically and economically and all with the involvement of the local community. It was the sort of creative approach that America's desperate inner-city poverty would require. His work in Bedford-Stuyvesant was testament to his instinct to match his inner passion with practical intervention.

Martin Luther King and Robert F. Kennedy were, each in their own way, trying to find ways to tackle America's deep and profound inequalities, both economic and racial. Dr King's final organisational effort was a Poor People's Campaign to demand both an increase in the rate and coverage of the minimum wage as well as a massive $30 billion anti-poverty package.

*Jack Newfield, p. 87.

The intention was for the campaign to culminate in a march on Washington. Like Moses, Dr King never did reach his destination and the campaign lost its drive. Instead, following his assassination in Memphis on April 4, 1968, America descended into another wave of urban violence.

It is unlikely that the Poor People's Campaign would have enjoyed any great success. Already, President Johnson was losing the political will to go any further with the anti-poverty crusade that had preoccupied him in the early part of his presidency. Besides, the economic wherewithal just wasn't there. The economic situation did not command a further expansion of expenditure and President Johnson's analysis of the causes of the riots differed greatly from those of Martin Luther King and Robert F. Kennedy. Moreover, he was already having difficulty getting the tax rises that he needed through Congress. The purpose of those tax rises was not the alleviation of poverty. It was to fund the Vietnam War.

A movement against war and poverty was coming together. It needed a leader and candidate for the presidential elections in 1968.

❧

A fair amount of cajoling went into persuading Kennedy to assume the leadership of a new popular movement. His reluctance throughout 1967 and the early part of 1968 meant that the different elements of this movement and even some of his staff, who had either left or taken sabbaticals, had attached themselves to the candidacy of Eugene McCarthy rather than risk the re-nomination of Lyndon Johnson.

While Senator McCarthy's anti-Vietnam War credentials were impeccable, his liberal record was far from unambiguous. McCarthy had voted both against a minimum wage for farm workers and to exclude a large number of workers from minimum wage legislation, against laws outlawing poll taxes, against limiting draft extensions, whilst siding with the National Rifle Association against gun control. He seemed, all things considered, to be a Peacenik candidate rather than a potential leader of a broad-based progressive movement and a intellectually haughty one at that. Americans for Democratic Action had given McCarthy a rating of 62 percent in 1967 while Kennedy's rating consistently hit 100 percent.*

In the spring of 1967, Allard Lowenstein, an anti-war activist from New York had begun a 'Dump Johnson' campaign. Lowenstein, a board member of Americans for Democratic Action, had a guiding ethos that mass mobilisation and grassroots organisation were key to removing President Johnson and putting a Democrat in the White House who would withdraw American forces from Vietnam. Kennedy was still thinking in terms of a presidential run in 1972 when Lowenstein tried to persuade him in 1967 that to run against Johnson was a winnable proposition. Kennedy was far from convinced.

---

*Joseph A Palermo, p. 80.

To rip apart the Democratic Party was foolhardy and to replace a sitting President was without recent precedent. His political heart may have led him in a different direction, but in 1967 the rational calculation that it was better to wait for 1972 still had a stronger pull.

Lowenstein would continue to build up the force of the anti-war movement in the coming months with the intention of putting together sufficient support to remove President Johnson. He mobilised 30,000 students to canvass against President Johnson, door to door, in the summer of that year, and later led a march of 50,000 anti-war demonstrators on the Pentagon. A National Conference for New Politics was organised in Chicago later that year with Martin Luther King as its keynote speaker.* This mobilisation, an attempt to build a grassroots front of resistance and replacement, was impressive but it was never going to be enough.

The movement was about to find a more convincing leader than Eugene McCarthy. Events in Vietnam in early 1968 ended the presidency of Lyndon Johnson and sent the 1968 election into a dizzying spin. The same month as the announcement of Eugene McCarthy's candidacy, General Westmoreland, Commander of US forces in Vietnam, bravely predicted before the National Press Club that a point had been reached in Vietnam where, 'the end comes into view.'

Breaking a traditional cessation in hostilities during the Tet (Lunar New Year) holiday in January 1968, the

---

*Joseph A Palermo, pp. 67–71.

National Liberation Front, more commonly referred to as the Vietcong, launched an offensive into the heart of South Vietnamese and American defences. It got as far as attacking General Westmoreland's headquarters and the US Embassy in Saigon.

If the immediate military shock of the offensive wasn't damaging enough, the fact that just two months previously General Westmoreland had been giving such an optimistic picture of the situation in Vietnam was deeply damaging for the President and his administration. Lyndon Johnson's approval ratings began to plummet. Worse was to come. Robert Kennedy was about to enter the fray and decisively so.

A speech that Kennedy gave to a Book and Author luncheon in Chicago on February 8, 1968, attended by Mayor Richard J. Daley amongst others, was to mark the beginning of an escalation against the President.

The Chicago speech in early 1968 was much more forceful and would take Kennedy almost to the point of no return. He rejected any notion that the US response to the Tet Offensive could be construed as a victory. America could not win where South Vietnam and her incompetent, corrupt government had failed. There was no military solution to what was essentially a cultural, historical and political problem. The catalogue of delusion, dishonesty and failure was already considerable. 'First the French and then the United States have been predicting victory in Vietnam. In 1961 and in 1962, as well as 1966 and 1967, we have been told that the "tide is turning"; there is "light at the end of the tunnel"; "we can soon bring home the troops – victory is near – the enemy is tiring." Once, in 1962, I participated in such predictions myself.'[*]

In conclusion, he stated: 'The best way to save our most precious stake in Vietnam – the lives of our soldiers – is to stop the enlargement of war.'[†] Kennedy was now diametrically against his own party's administration. The logical conclusion was a candidacy in the race for the Democratic nomination for President. The movement, after a year of persuasion, aided by events in the Vietnam War itself, finally had its leader. Kennedy was someone who could win the nomination *and had the potential to win an election also.*

On March 16th, Johnson's nightmare became reality. Kennedy entered the race, attacking the policies of the administration, when he declared: 'I run because it is now unmistakably clear that we can change these disastrous, divisive policies only by changing the men who are now making them. For the reality of recent events in Vietnam has been glossed over with illusions. The Report of the Riot Commission has been largely ignored … I cannot stand aside from the contest that will decide our nation's future and our children's future … At stake is not simply the leadership of our party and even our country. It is our right to moral leadership of this planet.'[‡]

---

[*]Joseph A Palermo, p. 124.

[†]Joseph A Palermo, p. 124.

[‡]Robert F Kennedy, *Announcement of Candidacy for President,* Washington, DC, March 16, 1968. Robert F Kennedy Memorial.

With approval for his handling of the Vietnam War at 26 percent and his overall approval rating at 36 percent, Lyndon Baines Johnson, the most proficient, contradictory, divisive, intermittently brilliant politician of his generation addressed the nation on March 31st.* 'With American sons in the fields far away, with America's future under challenge right here at home, with our hopes and the world's hopes for peace in the balance every day, I do not believe that I should devote an hour, or a day, of my time to any personal partisan causes. Or to any duties other than the awesome duties of this office – the Presidency of your country. Accordingly, I shall not seek, and I will not accept, the nomination of my party for another term as your President.'

Perhaps the greatest master of the art and skulduggery of politics had been defeated by this new grassroots movement, Ho Chi Minh and the Vietcong.

And so the mantle of the party machine was passed to Lyndon Johnson's vice-president, Hubert Humphrey. Once Kennedy had won California it was a straight fight, despite the persistence of Eugene McCarthy, for the Democratic nomination. History was denied a conclusion to that contest.

❧

Kennedy's coalition, his movement of African-Americans, students, the liberal middle-class, the less

---

*Jack Newfield, p. 243.

affluent working-class, and Latinos (especially those in unions such as Cesar Chavez's United Farm Workers), could have provided the foundation for a movement for change under the right inspirational leadership. It is difficult to predict that it would have done so, whether Kennedy's persona would have been enough to make such a coalition work in the tumultuous 1968 election.

The significance of Kennedy's movement is that it hinted at what could be achieved on the liberal left given a favourable wind. In 2009 the US remains committed to a war in Iraq despite the fact that its operations have largely been a failure despite recent successes; its economy, skewed towards the very wealthy, facing huge budget deficits and financial collapse, is in crisis; and a new set of issues around energy and the environment constitute a fundamental challenge. This time though, it was a Republican administration that faced responsibility for failure. Those elements that Kennedy was looking to mould into a movement for change are there today, and in greater numbers, as the US demography changes into something more professional, more diverse, less racially divided.

Barack Obama sits at Robert F. Kennedy's desk in the US Senate. He has inherited more than his desk. He has also inherited Kennedy's movement, along with the movement of Martin Luther King, one he has fused into a new movement for change. The movement dispersed but never disbanded, lay dormant but never died, quietly waiting its opportunity, the right time and the right leadership to take it further than Kennedy or Martin Luther King were able to. That is Barack Obama's opportunity.

Lyndon Baines Johnson is worth one final mention. Without his achievements on civil and voting rights there could have been no possibility of a movement for change. His 'Great Society' has had a lasting impact today not least through a provision such as Medicare which still saves and improves millions of lives. On January 20, 1973 Richard M. Nixon was inaugurated for a second term. The following day he announced the withdrawal from Vietnam and a new plan to dismantle the Great Society. On January 22, 1973, Johnson died alone from a fatal heart attack, his wife and daughters away from his ranch. The success of the long 1960s would not have been possible without Lyndon Baines Johnson, warts and all.

Over-reaching and exhausted, the movement of peace, civil rights and the war on poverty was replaced by something quite different. Richard M. Nixon showed how a conservative movement could work politically. Later, Ronald Reagan, George H. W. Bush, and his son George W. Bush would build on Nixon's reactionary coalition and the conservative movement. Republican Presidents have sat in the Oval Office for twenty-eight of the last forty years. They have done so on the back of the conservative movement. Even in defeat in 2008, it is a movement that is neither dead nor buried. It could be on the wane but it's not wise to bet on that just yet. In fact, it is the exemplar of effective movement politics in action.

2

Backlash

'We have seen the rise of a great cause and a powerful movement.'

Karl Rove, 2004.*

THE CONSERVATIVE MOVEMENT gestated in the bowels of reaction to the civil rights, anti-poverty and peace movements of the 1960s. Four decades on, it may only now be facing the limits of its ability to command political power and skew the entire machinery of US politics in favour of free market conservatism, a religious values-based ideology and a belief in a strong and interventionist US foreign policy.

Its very nature, that of a movement, is of clear interest because it is a model that has delivered power

*James Moore and Wayne Slater, *The Architect: Karl Rove and the Dream of Absolute Power*, p. 211.

effectively and, in so doing, has defined the politics of the last forty years. The conservative movement has been uniquely successful in motivating its supporters, creating clear dividing lines or 'positive polarisation' to aggregate votes and power, and turning ideas into practice. Philosophically, financially, organisationally, electorally, whatever measure of political effectiveness one chooses to adopt, the conservative movement has acted with a unity of purpose that has managed to solder its inherent internal contradictions.

Theoretically, it should be as fractious as any alternative on the left. Moulding together libertarians, big-government, militarist conservatives, and values-motivated religious conservatives has the feel of a temporary and expedient coalition. Instead, a brand of populist conservatism has turned what should be something fleeting into a formidable vote-harvesting machine.

In fact, just such a coalition had come together behind the Presidential candidacy of Senator Barry Goldwater in 1964. The leading light of the conservative movement, its political founding father, Goldwater was against civil rights legislation, for the reduction of government, against labour unions, and for confrontation with the USSR. He was a core base-motivating conservative Republican.

His election campaign was a disaster from the moment he declared in his Republican nomination acceptance speech: 'I would remind you that extremism in the defence of liberty is not a vice! And let me remind you also that moderation in the pursuit of justice is no virtue!'* Cue rapturous applause at the Convention in San Francisco, but cue also massive electoral defeat.

Lyndon Johnson ruthlessly exploited the sense that Senator Goldwater was some type of unhinged extremist, not least with the Daisy Girl ad, one of the most famous and devastating election advertisements of all time. A cute girl is shown counting the petals of a daisy only for the idyllic sequence to morph into the countdown for a nuclear attack and Armageddon. It wasn't only the Republicans who could play dirty in those days. Even Goldwater's campaign slogan 'In your heart, you know he's right' was parsed into 'In your guts, you know he's nuts' by the Johnson campaign.

President Johnson's victory was spectacular. Senator Goldwater won only six states, mainly in the Deep South, was defeated 61 percent to 39 percent, and lost by around sixteen million votes. The notion that Barry Goldwater's platform was a harbinger that would initiate a movement and would be the foundation for a period of Republican domination of the White House for forty years, would have seemed preposterous in 1964. Yet, as Karl Rove explained in his 'powerful movement' speech of 2004: in 1964, Democrats held 68 Senate seats, 296 House seats and 33 governorships. By George W. Bush's vibrant victory in 2004, everything had been reversed. Republicans held 55 Senate seats, 232 House seats and 28 governorships. And the

---

* Alfred S. Regnery, *Upstream: The Ascendance of American Conservatism*, p. 99.

Republicans had won seven of the last ten presidential elections.*

Hubris leads to nemesis and pride comes before a fall. Nonetheless, the world must have seemed just as rosy to the Democrats in 1964. Within four years they had fallen apart. The same fate was to befall the Bush Administration and the Republicans more widely by 2008. In the 2006 mid-term elections the House majority had almost exactly reversed in favour of the Democrats, the Senate was now tied, and it was the Democrats who emerged with 28 out of 50 governorships. Karl Rove's glee in 2004 was premature, but more fundamentally, the conservative movement was showing the first real signs of fracturing and therein lay an opportunity for a movement for change to take its place.

ॐ

There is one figure who spans the whole of the conservative movement, was its intellectual energiser, coalition-builder and inspirational light. That figure is not Ronald Reagan, who only really came on board in his 'time for choosing' speech of 1964. Nor is it Barry Goldwater, whose campaign was the first try-out for a new, conservative platform, and whose work, *The Conscience of a Conservative,* became the conservative bible.

William F. Buckley, conservative thinker, publisher, campaigner and leader, died on February 27, 2008,

---

*James Moore and Wayne Slater, p .211.

during the presidential primary campaigns. It was a salutary reminder of his contribution in defining an era of American politics. In 1955, he launched the *National Review*, which was to do more than perhaps any other publication to unify the disparate wings of modern populist conservatism. It was the ideas factory for a movement, and a decade or so later, following the Goldwater campaign, those ideas would start to gain traction.

As Alfred S. Regnery summarises it: 'Before they could become a movement, organised around practical policy positions, the traditionalists, libertarians and anti-Communists needed to work out their philosophical differences and find common philosophical principles as bases for joint practical action. It was eventually up to *National Review* to fuse these different positions into a unified whole.'*

It was Buckley and a group of other conservative activists who responded to the defeat of Barry Goldwater by establishing the American Conservative Union as a political action and lobbying organisation. Its essence was to ensure that it captured the spirit of Goldwater but it soon began to crystallise into something with greater political appeal and clout.

It is interesting that the practical response by these conservatives was not to ditch the strategy pursued by Barry Goldwater but instead to try to find a way to make it work. Almost any conventional political

---

*Alfred S. Regnery, p. 67.

analysis would suggest that a purist strategy that had led to abject defeat was doomed to repeat failure. Amazingly, Buckley's resolve resulted in success. He had put the building blocks in place. What made it a success, however, were the convulsions that were beginning to consume liberalism and, as it seemed to many 'Main Street' Americans, the nation also.

These Americans watched as America's cities were reduced to pitched street battles between the police and rioters; reacted with disgust at the horror and national humiliation that was evolving in Vietnam. They looked askance at a litany of other threats to their understanding of the American way: increasing radicalism in the civil rights movement ('Black Power' was lurking), an increase in crime, the breakdown of the traditional family, the growing numbers of elite students protesting against the institutions of the nation, and rising taxes to pay for much of this.

This more traditional America, middle-class, almost exclusively white, residing in small towns and suburbs, was not swayed by the 1960s. This was an America clinging desperately to the halcyon days of the 1950s, to a country that had liberated the world, and whose economy had delivered spectacular increases in living standards. Believers in the security of the traditional family and the job for life, God-fearing and committed to a certain way of life: whether billboard ad perfection or myth, this America looked on with disgust at a decade of social forces, previously tethered, becoming unleashed.

And worse, not only was the Federal government complicit in these changes, but, even more incredibly, the Supreme Court was in on the act too. *Brown v Board of Education, Topeka* was one thing, but then along came *Baker v Vintale,* under which officially-sponsored school prayer was declared unconstitutional, followed by *Miranda v Arizona,* under which criminal process and procedure for defendants was defined by the Warren Court. What about the victims of crime?

Then, particularly for America's large evangelical and Catholic populations, came the ultimate insult. In 1973, the national debate about abortion rights was abruptly and conclusively settled by the Supreme Court when *Roe v Wade* legally determined, at Federal rather than State level, that it was a woman's right to choose.

There was now a wider opportunity for a conservative movement. A neo-liberal, business-first philosophy was never going to have the political power of a message based around the perceived threat to one's core values. In the 1960s, a political platform designed around this narrow appeal to traditional America alone would never really equate to much more than the 27 million votes that Barry Goldwater received in 1964. What began to happen from the mid-1960s onwards was the birth of a new category of Republican. These voters were the real difference between the ability of the Republicans to secure power occasionally and govern for generations. They were what have become known as 'Reagan Democrats.'

The first inkling that there may have been a white

working-class backlash vote came in the mid-term elections of 1966. By this point the Civil Rights Act and Voting Rights Act and the subsequent civil disturbances had occurred. In April 1965, 71 percent of Americans said that the Johnson administration was 'pushing racial integration' either 'not fast enough' or 'about right.' Following the Watts riot of that year, that had changed to 52 percent who thought it was 'pushing too hard'.* That slide in support for continuing racial integration would continue throughout the decade. Its electoral impact was best characterised by the 1966 Senate race between Senator Paul L. Douglas and his Republican opponent, Charles Percy. In 1960 Douglas had won the state by a margin of 437,097 votes, including a 525,013 margin in Chicago. In 1966, after Martin Luther King's protests and the riots of the same year, white support for Douglas collapsed. Senator Douglas lost by 422,302 votes statewide and his margin amongst white voters in Chicago alone fell by 339,303 votes.†

The distinguishing feature of the Reagan Democrats is that they would be assumed to naturally vote Democrat. Collective government action, labour unions, government assistance, and tax and welfare policies aimed at lower income groups would seem, on the face if it, to be in their self-interest. On that reading, much of the American electorate votes against its own self-interest.

---

*Thomas Byrne Edsall with Mary D. Edsall, *Chain Reaction: The Impact of Race, Rights and Taxes on American Politics*, p. 59.
†Thomas Byrne Edsall with Mary D. Edsall, p. 60.

Thomas Frank, in his bestselling, *What's the Matter with Kansas?*, puts it well when he describes the appeal of populist conservatism: 'While earlier forms of conservatism emphasised fiscal sobriety, the *backlash* mobilises voters with explosive social issues – summoning public outrage over everything from busing to un-Christian art – which it then marries to pro-business economic policies. Cultural anger is marshalled to achieve economic ends. And it is these economic achievements – not the forgettable skirmishes of the never-ending culture wars – that are the movement's greatest monuments.'

Whether we accept that culture is a mask for economic interests or not, there is no doubting that Frank's ultimate conclusion is right. When we add in an anti-elitist hue to the mix, it becomes easier to see how people end up, paradoxically, voting Republican to show their displeasure with Wall Street: a sentiment that John McCain and Sarah Palin once again tried to mine in the presidential campaign of 2008.

There is a language of conservatism in America that is uniquely American. The cadences and political prose of the American liberal left is recognisably that of liberals or progressives elsewhere. American conservatism has some vague, thematic similarities with other branches of conservatism but in its populist rancour it is utterly different and more akin to what may be observed in New Right politics in Europe.

Conservatives in America, despite their formidable record of winning and holding on to power, still see themselves as the outsiders who are tasked with defending real American values. Fox News and the latitude of right-wing talk show hosts, magazines, direct mailings, think tanks, campaign groups, religious organisations and so on, constitute the modern, still-powerful conservative movement. Perhaps it would not exist at all had it not been for the tumultuous, long 1960s. Without a backlash, perhaps it would have remained a fringe concern limited to the *National Review*, a few campaigners, maverick members of Congress, religious activists, disgruntled Southern whites and suited entrepreneurs. It would, in other words, look like the Barry Goldwater campaign and be just as lacking in electoral force.

But that was not its fate. Instead it embarked on a strategy of 'positive polarisation' and built the most formidable political movement and national election-winning machine in US history. The election strategy was put into play for the first time by Richard Nixon's campaign of 1968. As Pat Buchanan, who worked for Richard Nixon, put it: 'From day one, Nixon and I talked about creating a new majority. What we talked about, basically, was shearing off huge segments of FDR's New Deal coalition, which LBJ had held together: Northern Catholic ethnics and Southern Protestant conservatives what we called the [Mayor] Daley-Rizzo Democrats in the North and, frankly, the Wallace Democrats in the South.'* The Nixon Administration aimed to polarise America into two opposite but unequal nations. One

---

*George Packer, *The New Yorker*, May 26, 2008.

was 'quiet, patriotic, religious, law-abiding' and the other 'noisy, elitist, amoral, disorderly and condescending.'*

'Positive polarisation' worked in 1968 but only just. Nixon still needed the helping hand of George Wallace, the Alabama Governor, who stood as a segregationist Independent candidate. He only won the election by 500,000 votes against Hubert Humphrey (amounting to a 301 to 191 electoral college victory), thanks to Wallace eating into the Democratic vote. In states that together could have swung the election to Humphrey, such as Illinois, Missouri and Ohio, Wallace's vote was greater than the margin between Nixon and Humphrey.

1968 marked the firing gun for the broadening of this strategy. Nixon applied some of the early techniques that had been innovated in the Goldwater campaign and would become the tried and tested weapons of the conservative ascendancy: fundraising from small donors through politically explosive direct mail and the voter mobilisation of new conservative grassroots organisations.† Already, Nixon secured almost 30 percent of unionised neighbourhoods in the election. The Democratic base was weakening and fast.

As it happened, Nixon's presidency was a major disappointment to conservatives. William F. Buckley was appalled with Nixon following his *rapprochement* with China. Nixon extended the reach of the regulatory state, something of an anathema to conservatives. He

---

*George Packer.
† Alfred S. Regnery, pp. 135–136.

created the Environment Protection Agency and he did it by Executive Order to boot. Other regulatory bodies that he established included the Consumer Product Safety Commission and the Occupational Safety and Health Administration, all this on top of the passing of the Clean Air Act in 1970. That he attempted to control wages and prices was a sin against neo-liberal economics. Social spending overtook defence expenditure for the first time in US history.* Clearly, Nixon felt that there was still a need for conservatives to stick to the middle ground, triangulating between a purist Buckley political creed and over-reaching liberals.

The Nixon presidency could have been just one more swing of the pendulum of a balanced national politics, and that is how it looked after his replacement Gerald Ford was defeated by the Southern Democratic Governor Jimmy Carter. Unseen, grassroots were sprouting and they would emerge then bloom into a national hegemony. In 1974, only 18 percent of voters were registered Republican and the party was not necessarily seen as a natural ally for average Joes everywhere. As the social critic Donald Critchlow wrote: 'The catalyst for this transformation was found in the grassroots reaction against feminism, legalized abortion, ERA [Equal Rights Amendment], and the ban on prayer in schools.'†

---

*John Micklethwait and Adrian Woolridge, p. 70, and Alfred S. Regnery, pp. 136–139.

†Alfred S. Regnery, p. 178.

Economic and global security concerns, around which American politics had been structured certainly since Franklin Roosevelt, had been replaced by social values, so-called 'culture wars', as a defining dynamic for American politics. It was Richard Nixon's campaign of 1968 that had begun this process in a serious way but it was driven beyond that dynamic by a movement comprising moralists, evangelicals, anti-interventionists and states' rightists that would begin to first reconfigure the nature of political exchange and then radically mobilise their base to secure electoral success.

In 1976, over 50 percent of all evangelicals voted for President Jimmy Carter.* By the 2004 presidential election, 80 percent of evangelical voters, comprising approximately 23 percent of the electorate, supported George W. Bush.† How could such a reconfiguration happen? It can only be explained by a reconfiguration of the axis of American politics.

The pollster Stanley Greenberg takes the example of Macomb County, Michigan to illustrate the success of the Republican strategy. Macomb is 90 percent white, 50 percent Catholic and 40 percent unionised. It is precisely the sort of county where issues such as race, cultural values, concerns about welfare and taxes, could have an impact. In 1960, Macomb was the most Democratic suburban county in the country with John F.

---

*Alfred S. Regnery, p. 164.
†CNN exit poll. http://edition.cnn.com/ELECTION/2004/pages/results/states/US/P/00/epolls.0.html

Kennedy securing 63 percent of the vote. Johnson bettered that. He secured 75 percent. By 1984, 66 percent of Macomb voters were supporting Ronald Reagan.* Macomb is both symbol of and testament to the success of the conservative movement.

A mixture of individual wealth, campaigning technique, moral or Christian fervour and tactical brilliance were responsible for this great political shift. Figures who were behind the success were those such as Richard Mellon Scaife, who has poured tens of millions of dollars into conservative causes such as the Heritage Foundation over the last four decades. His financing of the organised effort to root out President Bill Clinton's past, code-named the 'Arkansas Project', contributed to the attempt to impeach the President. When people talk about a 'vast right-wing conspiracy', it is Richard Mellon Scaife who is at the front and centre of their thinking. However, the conservative movement cannot be characterised as a 'conspiracy.' It is far too diffuse, its numbers far too great, its donors too numerous, for it to be described as a conspiracy. It is a highly effective movement and it is very visible.

By far the most powerful element of its armoury is the Christian political wing. This has changed in form over the years but its impact remains. Quite simply, the Christian thread of the conservative movement has

---

*Stanley B. Greenberg, James Carville, Andrew Baumann, Karl Agne, Jesse Contario, *Back to Macomb: Reagan Democrats and Barack Obama*, p. 1.

proved to be one the most effective vote-harvesting machines ever constructed. It is not just the numbers of voters it reaps for Republican candidates but the quality of the votes. Every vote is equal but some are more equal than others, particularly in swing states in a winner-takes-all electoral system.

In targeting voters who are both working-class and have religious conviction, states that should be Democratic strongholds become winnable for even right-wing Republican nominees (in general terms the more religious a voter is, measured by how often they attend a church service, the more susceptible they are to the religious right). The 'Reagan Democrats', reacting to welfare, taxes, culture and religious values can be picked away from their supposed natural socio-demographic terrain.

Ohio is the example often quoted in this regard but it is a bellwether state. Industrial Midwest Michigan is a far more interesting example. Areas such as Macomb County have meant that Michigan was won by the Republicans in every single Presidential election from 1972 until 1992; a remarkable fact for such a blue-collar state. With large Baptist and Catholic populations, Michigan has a susceptibility to the religious right onslaught.

And it was an onslaught. The Moral Majority led by Jerry Falwell was at the vanguard. It was *Roe v Wade* which had begun Jerry Falwell's transition from charismatic religious leader to political titan, a process aided by such figures as Paul Weyrich. It was also Weyrich, armed with the financial backing of the Coors brewery, who founded the Heritage Foundation and who met with Falwell in 1979 to establish the Moral Majority.

The political activities of the Moral Majority could have simply amounted to newsletters on tables at the back of churches but they were far more ambitious than that. It very quickly became the largest and most significant evangelical political organisation. By 1982 it had trained 100,000 pastors, Falwell's thoughts were being broadcast over three hundred plus radio stations, and it had raised over $10 million from a mailing list of 2 million people. Moreover, during the 1980 election, the Moral Majority registered as voters between 2 and 3 million evangelicals. Using the power of direct mail, which both delivers highly targeted messages and raises significant finance if done well, the Moral Majority became a political force. It was with the help of the direct mail guru, Paul Viguerie, that Falwell was able to assist Ronald Reagan's election in that year.*

Working alongside the religious right was the moralist and anti-feminist right epitomised by Phyllis Schlafly. Her particular reactionary cause was opposition to the adoption of the Equal Rights Amendment, a seemingly innocuous constitutional amendment. By the time Phyllis Schlafly had mobilised an army of women against the amendment, you could have been mistaken for thinking that it was singularly responsible for the collapse of every value that Americans held dear.

---

*Alfred S. Regnery, pp. 168–169.

The irony that as a wife, mother, lawyer, and political and social activist, she should be lecturing the nation on traditional family values did not faze her in the slightest. She was on a roll and more responsible than perhaps any other person for preventing the adoption of the Equal Rights Amendment. More importantly, she used that issue to promulgate a broader concern and to tap into more basic fears. Gay rights, abortion and the counter-culture were all sucked into her analysis of an America that was on the wrong track.

Both the religious and social strands of the conservative movement were not mere flashes in the pan. In fact, the Moral Majority would collapse into an even more formidable vote aggregation machine: Ralph Reed's Christian Coalition. The explosive growth of the Christian Coalition would win elections for Republicans and help the party to recover from its 1992 election defeat to Bill Clinton. In running for the nomination of the Republican Party, Reverend Pat Robertson had amassed an organisation and a mailing list of millions of Christian voters. The question was what to do with such a resource. In 1989, a young political activist took the reins of the Christian Coalition and built it into an even more formidable machine than Falwell, Weyrich and Viguerie had achieved with the Moral Majority.

By the end of his first year, Ralph Reed had built an organisation with 57,000 members. By 1997, it had 1.9 million members and had been instrumental in the 1994 mid-term elections fought by Republicans on a purist, conservative platform, 'Contract with America.' The Coalition distributed 33 million voter guides in that race and exit polls showed that 88 percent of churchgoing white evangelicals cited 'family values' as a major factor in how they voted.*

Through volunteers, newsletters, direct mail, voter registration, formidable fundraising backed up by a network of publishers, TV channels and radio shows, the religious right was a crushing force in electoral politics in the Reagan/Bush years and would be so again under George W. Bush.

When combined with the ruthless electioneering of the Republican machine, the religious right would mobilise an army of voters. Lee Atwater, campaign manager for George H. W. Bush in 1988, and creator of the infamous Willie Horton ad which combined the fears of race, crime and more broadly liberalism, was the first grand master of Republican movement electioneering.

Atwater was not the last. The movement combined with Republican strategists was a frightening force. Where Lee Atwater went, Karl Rove was to follow. Master and apprentice harnessed the movement and used it for their political ends. Rove's apotheosis was the 2004 election. In 2000, it had been a strategic necessity for George W. Bush to present himself as a 'compassionate conservative.' In 2004, Karl Rove was unleashed.

Back in 1988, George W. Bush had been the George H. W. Bush campaign liaison with Christian conservatives.

---

*John Micklethwait and Adrian Woolridge, pp. 111–112.

It was a role in which he excelled by all accounts.* Now his re-election in 2004 was dependent upon the ability of the religious right to mobilise its masses on his behalf. The swing state in 2004 was Ohio with its 20 electoral votes being the difference between electoral victory and defeat. Just 60,000 votes swinging from Bush to John Kerry would have meant a Democrat in the White House. The success of the religious right more than accounted for that number of votes. To mobilise its voters, there needed to be a blue touch-paper issue. That issue was gay marriage.

Fortuitously for Rove, Ohio had a plebiscite on its ballot that year to outlaw any marriage that was not a union between a man and a woman through a state constitutional amendment. The measure was called 'Issue One.' Rove used this to his advantage. As Phil Burris of the Cincinnati-based Citizens for Community Values said: 'Bush would not have won without Ohio, and he would not have won Ohio without Issue One.'†

Karl Rove knew that he had his work cut out for him in Ohio. The 2000 election had seen a drop off in the turnout in heavily Republican precincts and that had to be reversed if his President was to be returned to the White House. He set about a voter mobilisation strategy of which Issue One was a core component. As Republican pollster, Matthew Dowd, who worked on the campaign with Karl Rove has said: 'In 2000, we spent 75

---

*James Moore and Wayne Slater, p. 23.
†James Moore and Wayne Slater, p. 46.

percent of our resources on persuasion. In 2004, we spent 75 percent of all resources on motivation.'* Karl Rove was not prepared to simply rely on the evangelical vote. He also intended to widen George W. Bush's appeal to a broader catchment of religious voters.

Just over two million of Ohio's eleven and a half million population is Catholic. In 1998, the magazine *Crisis* had commissioned a study into Catholic voting behaviour. It found that though there was a Catholic vote there were also two conceptions of 'Catholic.' One was Catholic as an ethnic grouping tending to vote in line with its socio-economic status. The other was the churchgoing Catholic, analysis of whose voting behaviour revealed it to be a more values-driven demographic.† With the right tone, candidate and message, there was a potential appeal to these voters based around more traditional values.

Deal Hudson, the publisher of *Crisis*, became an outside adviser to the Bush campaign in 2000. In 2004, his outreach organisation, focusing on Catholic voters, began coordinating with Ralph Reed's Christian coalition to form a powerful and targeted political pincer movement. This was supplemented by doubts fermented about Kerry by the Swift Boat Veterans for Truth and Progress. The Swift Boat Veterans questioned Kerry's Vietnam War record and spent $8 million on TV advertising in Ohio alone.‡ Coordinated with ads

---

*James Moore and Wayne Slater, p. 81.

† Peter J Boyer, *The New Yorker*, September 8, 2008.

‡ James Moore and Wayne Slater, p. 86.

showing Kerry windsurfing and accusing him of 'flip-flopping' on the Iraq War, there was ample material for Bush to close the deal.

Pulling together the threads of a conservative movement comprising evangelicals, cultural conservatives and Catholics, their concerns energised by issues such as gay marriage, and their doubts stoked by questions around the Democratic candidate's patriotism and judgement, this machine delivered Ohio for Bush and secured for him a second term in the White House. It was just the latest success of a movement spanning President Nixon and President George W. Bush. The history of the late twentieth century Presidency is congruent with the history of the conservative movement.

Just as 1968 saw the liberal movement exhausted, over-reaching and destined to crumble, so it was for the conservative movement in 2008. The election victory of 2004 was perhaps the last time for a while that the Republicans could run a red-blooded conservative campaign and win. Having realised the increasing limitations of such a campaign in 2000, Bush had to run as a 'compassionate conservative.' Following the terrorist attacks of September 11, 2001, he had re-branded himself as a wartime leader in a 'War on Terror.' The base was charged up but Bush's victory was still incredibly narrow hinting at the underlying change in the American electorate that was to come to fruition in 2008.

By the end of his presidency, George W. Bush had not simply riled liberals but he had also dismayed his own side. He had expanded government expenditure to the point where the US now has an enormous Federal deficit. He had instituted government programmes such as No Child Left Behind and a Medicare prescription benefit. His presidency became defined by the neoconservative wing of the movement leading him into an extremely costly and unnecessary war in Iraq. By the end of his term of office, the image and reputation of the United States abroad had never been lower. Its financial system was collapsing requiring a $700 billion bailout of financial institutions and the nationalisation of a number of others. His presidency felt more akin to that of Richard Nixon than that of the hero of the conservative movement, Ronald Reagan.

The forces of structural change and monumental political failure would combine to present the most serious and potentially cataclysmic challenge to the conservative hegemony in forty years. The challenge was ideological, contextual, demographic and organisational. What was needed to break the grip of the movement was a strong counter movement waged by the Democrats. Such a movement was gestating in many ways in many different places. Most crucially, the spirit of the 1960s civil rights movement had been kept alive in a northern Midwestern city. That city was Chicago and its politics was about to be projected onto the national stage. The lead man was Barack Obama. He was performing new lines but the play had been in production for decades. It was now ready for public performance.

3

Chicago

*'Barack Obama started out as a community organizer
on the South Side of Chicago. He saw firsthand on
the ground the challenges that you face trying to get
government to work for the people, and so I think that
grounding will serve him well.'*

Valerie Jarrett, co-chair of President-elect Obama's

transition team.*

BULL CONNOR-STYLE southern segregationists could
have learned something from their racist cousins in Chicago. Like many American cities, Chicago is deeply segregated with its African-American population living in
the city's South and West sides. Its Latino population lives
on the city's Lower West side in areas such as Pilsen. This
city, though there have been improvements of late, still

Meet the Press, MSNBC, November 9, 2008.

bears the scars of wave after wave of migrants attempting to pull up the drawbridge before the next arrived. Its architecturally spectacular lake-fronting central business hub, The Loop, shimmers and deflects another reality. Once you leave that area, very quickly visitors find themselves in a series of mono-ethnic enclaves.

The official line is that this segregation, which in many instances amounts to ghettoisation, is voluntary, simply communities wanting to congregate. This doesn't hold up to any scrutiny. Chicago's segregation is a conspiracy lasting many decades. It involves commercial services, including real estate, credit providers and employers, public housing authorities, majority community resistance, political encouragement and legislation, and historical embedding of discriminatory action. By the time you hit Sox-35th on the Red Line going South, the mono-ethnicity of Chicago's South Side is patently obvious.

Whereas in the Deep South there was a straightforwardness about racial segregation, in Chicago there often has been denial. Historically, when there has been outrage at the conditions faced by certain groups, political forces briefly rise from their slumber to throw some resources or attention at the problem, only to go back to the old way of doing things once the dust has settled.

Epitomised but by no means limited to the tenure of Mayor Richard J. Daley who 'bossed' the city from 1957 until 1976, politicians would first deny that there was an issue. When they could deny no longer the claim that they were doing something about it, they would theatrically respond; before long, they and the city would move on to the next thing. As Martin Luther King would discover, much to his chagrin on his arrival in Chicago in 1966, it was a strategy just as enduring as anything devised by the confrontational South.

In a city where Latinos and African-Americans are significant minorities but neither comprises a majority, in the absence of cross-ethnic solidarity, swinging power in their favour for any period of time requires political feats that have only occasionally proved possible. One such time, perhaps the only time in almost a century of major African-American presence in Chicago (and this despite Chicago being founded by a black Haitian, Jean Baptiste Pointe du Sable), was during the painfully short tenure of Harold Washington from 1983 until he died, at his desk in the Mayor's fifth floor offices in City Hall, in 1987.

Washington was an inspiration. Not only that, he built around himself the type of city movement that, with the right leadership, could have provided more of an independent counter-balance to a new Daley machine, that of Richard M. Daley. Mayor Daley is not the same as his father and deserves independent assessment – he has been better for the city's African-American population than his father ever was – but his political instincts are just as ruthless.

He has been able to divide the African-American community and co-opt large parts of the Latino community to ensure that no coalition of minorities can challenge his position. Washington, who had electrified a people, a city both for and against his success, left it demoralised and deflated on his death. A community that had seen riots after the assassination of Martin Luther King was left to despair at how many great leaders had been taken from American politics before reaching their absolute prime.

Despite recent improvements in the city, for which Richard M. Daley deserves credit, Chicago is still deeply divided with pockets of quite shocking poverty. When Barack Obama arrived there in 1985, whole communities had been decimated by the huge loss of manufacturing employment. Though there had been a decline for quite some time this seemed to accelerate in the late 1970s and, more severely, during the Reagan years.

Manufacturing jobs in Chicago peaked at 668,056 in 1947. Between 1967 and 1982, there was a sharp decline. 46 percent, equating to a quarter of a million manufacturing jobs, were lost. Even worse, between 1972 and 1983 45,000 other jobs disappeared in the city whilst in the same period 316,000 jobs were added in the suburbs.* Even today, those shock waves reverberate in Chicago. Jesse Jackson said recently: 'Right now, you go northwest, there's, like, three jobs for every one person. If you go south, there's six people for every one job.'†

The pain of economic restructuring was not evenly

---

*Pierre Clavel and Wim Wiewel, *Harold Washington and the Neighbourhoods: Progressive City Government in Chicago, 1983– 1987,* p. 19.

†David Bernstein, *Chicago Magazine,* September 2008.

distributed. Separate is never equal and the largely ethnically homogenous communities of Chicago's South Side bore the brunt of economic change. Jobs with benefits became jobs that were temporary. Working families became welfare dependent. Communities that were economically active became repositories of despair. There wasn't necessarily anything malicious in this but that is hardly the point. By putting certain groups of people out on a dinghy, they were more exposed to the storm when it came. It came, and whole sections of the city were left without hope. The gangs were moving in, the schools were inadequate to the task, the police gave up, politicians evaded, families collapsed under the weight of hardship, and whole communities sank. It sounds dramatic but that was the cold, hard reality of industrial change for many of Chicago's ghettoes or ethnic islands.

It was to one of these ethnic islands that Barack Obama arrived in 1985. He had been employed by the Developing Communities Project run by Jerry Kellman, to work in and around the Roseland and Calumet areas of Chicago. Inspired by Harold Washington and the writings of another Chicagoan, Saul Alinsky, Barack Obama arrived with a sack of theory but very little practical experience. Over the next three years he would work on correcting that. It seems that the community which left the strongest impression on him is the enclave of Altgeld Gardens, a neighbourhood established for African-American soldiers returning from the Second World War (yes, even Franklin Delano Roosevelt's army was segregated).

The Altgeld Gardens experience cannot have left anything but a strong impression on Barack Obama. It is clear from his understanding of the gap between African-Americans and white Americans that he sees continuing disparity as both an inheritance from segregation combined with the impact of an economy that leaves millions of American citizens behind. In Altgeld Gardens he grew to understand what that meant in practice and began to appreciate exactly how he could deploy his talents to help people more effectively.

He saw the type of Chicago that seventeen years previously had drawn the admiration of Bull Connor. The man who had turned the fire hoses and dogs on protesters in Birmingham, Alabama, was appreciative of all that had been achieved in Chicago. When anti-war protesters were attacked by the Chicago Police Department in what an official Commission described as a 'police riot', it so resonated that when it came to Vice-Presidential nominations at the 1968 Chicago Convention, Bull Connor decided to show his appreciation for Mayor Richard J. Daley. He cast his vote for Daley as Hubert Humphrey's running mate though Daley was not even proposed for the ticket.* Chicago's surreptitious racism had its gong from the personification of Southern overt racism. Events in Chicago over the next fifteen years would show that acknowledgement to be richly deserved.

---

*Mike Royko, *Boss: Richard J. Daley of Chicago,* p. 193.

✤

Barack Obama describes the fundamental values that drove him in his time in Roseland, Chicago as, 'Issues, action, power, self-interest.'* These are precisely the values that would enable him to adopt a practical approach to the people on Chicago's South Side. Outcomes were what mattered to him: 'The continuing struggle to align word and action, our heartfelt desires with a workable plan – didn't self-esteem finally depend on just this? It was that belief which had led me into organising, and it was that belief which would lead me to conclude, perhaps for the final time, that notions of purity – of race or of culture – could no more serve as the basis for the typical black American's self-esteem than it could be mine.'†

For all the seductiveness of much of Malcolm X's early rage, Barack Obama was decisively moving in the direction of Martin Luther King. Jerry Kellman, the man who established the Developing Communities Project and gave Barack Obama his break in community organising, has no doubt the intellectual and practical insights that Obama was experiencing would have a profound effect on his personal and political future. On reading the first volume, titled *Parting the Waters,* of Taylor Branch's Pulitzer Prize winning history of the civil rights movement, *America*

---

*Barack Obama, *Dreams from My Father*, p. 155.
†Barack Obama, p. 204.

in the King Years, Obama confided in Kellman: 'This is my story.'*

Kellman felt this had a ring of truth to it. Some, looking at Obama's campaign in 2008, might reach for easy labels such as 'post-racial.' These descriptions would absolutely miss the point. Barack Obama's entire adult life has been defined neither by racial exclusivity nor racial detachment. Lazy and outdated concepts that were more useful a generation or more ago have been discarded and replaced by a modern sensitivity to the black American experience. Barack Obama, far from being beyond race, understands its history, its reality, but seeks to build a broad response to all of America's inequalities, so that no one injustice, however grave, is elevated above all others.

For Kellman, 'Barack has become the expectation of his people. And in that sense he is similar to King ... I think he knows that if he wants to go where he wants to go in politics, he has to speak for more than the black community. But I think the rest of his life, he will take on that burden of being the person who changes the situation for African-Americans.'†

That explains why Barack Obama was so readily able to reject the much of the thinking of Malcolm X. Black nationalism could only fail. It is impractical for separation to have any success because the reality of living in a community, in a nation, is that you can't get by other

---

*David Mendell, *Obama: From Promise to Power*, p. 73.
†David Mendell, p. 74.

than through cooperating with others. If the terms on offer in the black-owned bank are worse than those on offer elsewhere, is the small business owner meant to just swallow that? How can black society shut itself off, not work with white people, not shop in white stores? The realities are different. Black nationalism was an easy option for those looking for someone to blame. It had a ready market because it was clear and objectified grievance. Without cooperation and compromise, however, African-Americans were never going to improve their situation. Regardless of its affirmative message of solidarity and discipline, black nationalism was a blind alley and one into which Barack Obama would not stray. Instead, he arrived in Chicago ready to empower local communities by putting some of the thoughts of another Chicagoan in practice – Saul Alinksy.

Jerry Kellman was a disciple of Saul Alinsky and Obama's interest would certainly have done no harm in securing him a job in Chicago for $10,000 with a $2,000 car allowance. He had already shown an interest in Chicago in writing to Harold Washington's office in search of a job. He received no reply to that. When quizzed by Kellman about what he knew about Chicago he mentioned that he knew it was America's most segregated city and that 'white people' didn't like the fact that Harold Washington had become Mayor.* Moving to Chicago would be an entire new direction to Obama's life. He had decided not to drift anymore

---

*Barack Obama, p. 142.

but define his destiny. That destiny was in community organising; giving back and making a difference in his 20s outlook.

Obama was soon to discover just how infuriatingly segregated in mindset Chicago could be. Early in his time there he met one of the local pastors to try to engage him with the Developing Communities Project. The project had been established by a number of churches, including a number of Catholic churches, to help build the capacity of local communities to secure a better deal for themselves. Obama, as is the organiser's first brief, was looking to expand the organisation and his main strategy in achieving that was to woo more local churches. A 'Reverend Smalls' (Barack Obama mostly uses false names in his early memoir, *Dreams from My Father*) was fiercely defensive of his turf.

He rejected Obama's approach: 'Listen, Obama, you may mean well. I'm sure you do. But the last thing we need is to join up with a bunch of white money and Catholic churches and Jewish organisers [referring to Jerry Kellman] to solve our problems. They're not interested in us. Shoot, the archdiocese in this city is run by stone-cold racists. Always has been. White folks come in here thinking they know what's best for us, hiring a buncha high-talking, college-educated brothers like yourself who don't know no better, and all they want to do is take over.'*

That reaction could just be dismissed as parochialism,

---

*Barack Obama, p. 161.

and it certainly contained an element of that. There was more to it, however. War-weary, imbued with lazy assumptions about the nature of his congregation's struggle, and unwilling to reach out the hand of trust to those who might be able to make a difference, 'Reverend Smalls' was happy to rest on comfortable received wisdom rather than seeking new possibilities. It could be described as naïve black nationalism. It wasn't that. It embodied some of the assumptions of black nationalism without tapping into its vital energy. It represented the precise antithesis of what Obama was trying to achieve. The principles of Saul Alinsky could not have been further from the thinking of 'Reverend Smalls.'

In one of the stranger coincidences of the Democratic primary campaign in 2008, Barack Obama and Hillary Clinton shared a common, youthful passion for the philosophy and writing of Saul Alinsky. Hillary Rodham Clinton had written her senior thesis at Wellesley College on Alinsky, giving it the belligerent title, 'There is only the fight …'. In fact, Saul Alinsky had offered Hillary Rodham a job in 1968 while she was writing the thesis.* She didn't take him up on the offer. Both Obama and Clinton ditched the more confrontational elements of Alinsky but their youthful interest in him speaks to his power on activists and organisers from the 1960s up to the current day. In fact, as a result of Barack Obama's success, expect a mini-revival of the

---

*Peter Slevin, *Washington Post*, March 25, 2007.

Alinsky method and a growth of community organising as a vocation and endeavour.

There are so many causes that bear Saul Alinsky's fingerprints. Perhaps his earliest endeavours in the Back of the Yards neighbourhood in the 1930s are his most famous. He organised this deprived community (made famous by Upton Sinclair's novel, *The Jungle*) into an organisation of organisations – church, community and trade unions – and led successful strikes, pickets and boycotts. Beyond that, he mobilised the workers of Rochester, New York against the discriminatory practices of the industrial giant, Eastman Kodak, which was by far the largest local employer. Arriving in Rochester in 1965, the year after the riots, he was instantly accused of meddling by Kodak.

Asked what he thought of Rochester by the local newspaper, he bluntly replied: 'It a huge southern plantation transplanted north.' Using characteristic wit, a well-worn but devastatingly effective tactic in his armoury, he responded, when asked what he thought about the work that Kodak had done for black workers in Rochester: 'Maybe I am innocent and uninformed of what has been happening here, but as far as I know the only thing that Eastman Kodak has done on the race issue in America has been to introduce colour film.'*

It was during the course of this campaign that Alinsky worked with Robert F. Kennedy, then New York

---

*Saul Alinsky, *Rules for Radicals: A Pragmatic Primer for Realistic Radicals*, p. 137.

Senator, of whom he said: 'In my discussions with Kennedy, I found that his commitment was not political but human. He was outraged by the conditions in the Rochester ghetto.'*

In Chicago, Alinsky helped to establish the Woodlawn Organisation. Woodlawn is a neighbourhood in Chicago that had become ghettoised, the white population having fled the area as it became multi-racial in the 1950s. By the 1960s, it was yet another Chicago South Side community that was mono-ethnically black. There was a clear tension between the leadership of the Woodlawn Organisation and Saul Alinsky but there were notable successes also. The major threat to the community was the expansion of the University of Chicago. Alinsky was bolstered within the mainly African-American community of Woodlawn by the University's personal attacks on him. If he wasn't a threat to the University's plans, why would they by attacking him? He used the credibility that secured for him to great effect.

By fusing a range of groups and interests, the same technique used in the Back of Yards organisation, the Woodlawn Organisation managed to get the city of Chicago to issue a new policy statement on urban renewal. (The policy granted all five of the Woodlawn Organisation's demands.) Alinsky was pleased to see the organisation's leaders refuse to accept second best when they stormed into his office, infuriated at how *little* City Hall had offered them. He remarked wryly: 'They were

---

*Saul Alinsky, p. 174.

fighting for hamburger; now they wanted filet mignon; so it goes. And why not?'*

It was not just by Alinsky's practical successes, impressive though they were, that the likes of Barack Obama and Hillary Clinton were most inspired. It was his ethos that was of most use to the aspirant community organiser.

Alinsky's philosophy was one of practical revolution. He was appalled by ideological dogma. He writes in *Rules for Radicals*: 'This is not an ideological book expect insofar as argument for change, rather than for the status quo, can be called ideology; different people, in different places, in different situations in different times will construct their own solutions and symbols of salvation for those times.'† His sole ideological commitment was that for change in favour of the have-nots. His method was whatever it took to achieve that end.

The way forward was to organise. The young would need to become organisers, developing all the skills that would entail. For the organiser, truth is changing and relative, not fixed and dogmatic. A successful organiser must be a political realist. Alinsky wrote: 'The basic requirement for the understanding of the politics of change is to recognise the world as it is.'‡ The world is defined by perceived self-interest, it is a place where power decides outcomes. The 'haves' will do anything

---

*Saul Alinsky, p. 107.
†Saul Alinsky, p. 4.
‡Saul Alinsky, p. 12.

possible to maintain the status quo; the 'have-nots' might seem fatalistically despairing but can be mobilised given the right circumstances and organisation; and the 'have-a-little, want mores', the middle-class, have one foot in the change camp and a firmer foot in the status quo.

Alinsky thought that the future was in the fusion of the interests of the 'haves' and the 'have-a-little, want mores.' It was to this latter group, with a focus on the white middle-class, that his interest turned in the latter years of his life. His fear was that if this group's needs and interests were not met then, motivated by the fear of the 'red menace' or of the breakdown of law and order, they would turn to George Wallace, the John Birch Society or other right-wing groupings. His concerns proved to be prescient, demonstrating an understanding of the forces that led to the phenomenon of the 'Reagan Democrats.' He wrote: 'If we don't win [the lower middle-class], Wallace or Spiro T. Nixon (*sic*) will.'*

Perhaps in an echo of Alinsky's view that, 'Insecure in this fast-changing world, they cling to illusory fixed points – which are very real to them,'† Barack Obama made his controversial 'bitter' comments. Speaking at a fundraiser in San Francisco, he told his audience, in reference to small-town America: 'It's not surprising that they get bitter. They cling to gin or religion or antipathy to people who aren't like them or anti-immigration

---

*Saul Alinsky, p. 189.
†Saul Alinsky, p. 188.

sentiment or anti-trade sentiment as a way to explain their frustrations.'*

Whether the communities were the poor black neighbourhoods of Chicago, exploited meat-trade workers, or the newly dispossessed and disempowered lower middle-class, the mission was the same. The organiser must listen to people's needs intently, mobilise them around definable causes, deploy the right tactics in achieving the mission, then ensure that the authority, organisation or commercial enterprise responsible followed through on its commitments. To achieve this, the organiser could not shy away from words that the rest of us may see as negative. He must know and use power; understand self-interest and mobilise it, channel it; understand the art of compromise, fundamental as it is to the nature of a free and open society; use and appreciate his ego as a creative force; and understand how to use conflict to secure his ends.

Alinsky cites the example of the civil rights movement in the South that used passive resistance and commercial pressure to fight the segregationists, and won. Such an understanding of the *particular* means that will secure *particular* ends was necessary for the success of the cause.

By the time he left Altgeld Gardens, Obama had seen the limitations of community organising in the pursuit of change. Political leaders could achieve far more with their signature on a law than was possible in the years of

---

*Mayhill Fowler, *Huffington Post,* April 11, 2008.

hard work that people like him devoted to community organising. He was determined to make a difference, to initiate change, and in that he has never deviated from the core Alinsky philosophy. To that extent, Alinsky's influence on the Barack Obama who ran for President in 2008 is clear. He would eschew some of his more confrontational tactics but surely Alinsky's ethos of active citizens mobilising to change their world rather than simply settling for a deeply unsatisfactory status quo is at the core of Obama's movement for change.

In 1985, Barack Obama was yet to understand the difference he could make in a community setting. Ultimately, the frustration grew that his victories were won while swimming against the tide. The question of how to change the tide was for another day. When he arrived in Altgeld Gardens, the question was how he could help to prevent a community from sinking altogether.

❦

Linda Randle possesses a wicked sense of humour. She has the ability to cut you down with a single flash of her golden eyes. Were she 'connected', she would be the one who could tell you where the bodies were buried. She is an oracle and a force of nature. It is not too difficult to imagine the fear of an administration clerk in City Hall on hearing that a phone message had been left by Linda or, even worse, that Linda was to visit.

Linda understands every aspect of Altgeld Gardens, where she has lived for the past two decades. No block is unexplored; no door is closed to Linda. She worked with Barack Obama on the asbestos campaign in the late 1980s. Her own patch was the Ida B. Wells project near to The Loop, round about 37th Street on Chicago's South Side. It was there she discovered that the housing had been constructed using asbestos. Her campaign would later serve as a model for that which Barack Obama was to establish with the residents of Altgeld Gardens. They met through an umbrella organisation, Community Renewal Society, which community organisers would use to exchange experiences and stories about the challenges they were facing.

As a public servant and political activist, Linda has seen it all. Nowadays, she's not too steady on her legs but is always with her 'husband', a walking stick that steadies her legs as her mind works over-time. She lived in Altgeld Gardens from the early 1990s and saw a community, already on its knees, decline further.

She is clear on the plight of the neighbourhood: 'Altgeld Gardens is the worst community in Chicago no doubt. At least where there is poverty and deprivation elsewhere there are programmes to deal with it and other communities are more mixed. But not Altgeld Gardens.'

'The only thing is to suspend your rational responses when it comes to Altgeld. None of your rational instincts work. You need to just catch your breath and try to contemplate the enormity of it.'

Linda now lives in the regeneration area in the vicinity of Cellular Field, the Chicago White Sox stadium, round about 35th Street. That area has a feeling of uplift to it. New low-rise flat developments mix tenure, both public and private; new retail facilities and offices ensure that there is local employment and enterprise; it is the very model of modern urban regeneration. Quite apart from the shining beacon of the new baseball stadium, the area has the bustle and optimism that comes with a community going in the right direction. Nearby, Lake Park is being regenerated in a similar fashion.

These developments are all in the ward of Alderman Toni Preckwinkle, a fearless and independent politician who has fought for the comprehensive overhaul of local communities that were crime ridden, over-crowded, deprived, and unfit for human habitation. She is a fierce critic of the concept of 'rehabilitation', which is exactly what is occurring in Altgeld Gardens. Rehabilitation involves the housing authority, in this case the Chicago Housing Authority, refurbishing homes. From a physical perspective it is very welcome. From a broader community perspective, what often happens is that while the physical character and comfort of an area is improved the communities remain the same. To oversimplify slightly, you end up with the same mix of social problems but in a more pleasant setting.

Alderman Preckwinkle said: 'Rehabs don't work. You have to completely rebuild communities. My ward has done well from transformation money. Transformation is far more effective than rehabbing.'

The one negative impact, however, is that many lower-income families are forced out of an area when it is transformed. One of the features of poor urban housing is its high density. When that density is reduced and the area is simultaneousness economically uplifted many people are forced out and it tends to be those with the fewest means. Though in itself not an argument against transformation it is a process that has to be carefully managed. Where do those who have to move out go? A variety of places – a deprived area like Altgeld Gardens being one of them. This process has not been managed properly with predictable outcomes in Altgeld Gardens as new deprived families meet an existing deprived population.

Ward 4 is an exemplar of the energising impact of urban transformation. Altgeld Gardens demonstrates, in Ward 9 and in contrast, the limits of rehabilitation. The area is currently mid-way through a process of redevelopment.

Linda's warning about the need to 'suspend your rational responses' is very good advice. The first thing to strike you about Altgeld Gardens is that, physically, it does not seem too bad. Sure, a lot of the houses are boarded up, but that is because of the ongoing building works. Altgeld Gardens stretches from East 131st to East 133rd Street east of Langley Avenue. The houses are arranged into square-shaped blocks. This can have two results. In a square, with forty or fifty houses arranged in close proximity, good community values can be reinforced, or anti-social behaviour can quickly spread, forcing people back into the privacy of their own homes and causing a breakdown in community.

Standing in one of the blocks, it is easy to imagine a thriving neighbourhood with the kids playing, each looking out for each other's family and property. A social hubbub could give the place a buzz, a community feel that once Altgeld Gardens actually had and often still does but in less visible ways.

It would seem that the local alderman (councillor), Anthony Beale, has failed to win the confidence of the people of Altgeld Gardens. In fairness to him, the big decisions affecting the area were taken well before he was in office. While some areas of Chicago were transformed, Altgeld Gardens was simply rehabilitated.

Perhaps it's his behaviourist approach that some find off-putting. For example, Alderman Beale said: 'We have to change the mindset of the community. You have to get people to start believing in themselves. I am a prime example of what can be achieved. I started out in these communities, then worked my way up and got a good corporate job. Now I represent the local community. The problems in Altgeld are not just in Altgeld. They are throughout the entire community. You have to go where the jobs are. You have to just go out and get it.'

However, if it were a simple matter of individual behaviour then the type of comprehensive transformation that is occurring elsewhere in Ward 4 would not be necessary.

These decisions were taken long before Alderman Beale was on the scene but it is clear that the deeply embedded issues faced in Altgeld are not simply going to be resolved even by investing hundreds of millions of dollars in rehabilitation. The fissure between Alderman Beale and the people of Altgeld may have its roots in the decision of a local resident, Harold 'Noonie' Ward, to stand against him in 2007. At that time, Alderman Beale had fallen out with his political sponsor Reverend James Meeks, the State Senator for the Illinois 15th District. The rift was healed and Alderman Beale won.

Reverend Meeks himself was causing quite a stir in the local community in early September 2008. He had just organised a schools boycott on the first day of term. School funding in Illinois has long been contentious as it is based on local taxes. What this means in practice is that wealthier counties have better financed education, better teachers, better facilities, and, consequently, better results. In the context of a city such as Chicago that is heavily segregated, this crazy way of financing local education harms particular ethnicities, such as the African-American and Latino communities, who live in its more deprived parts. So Reverend Meeks' cause was an absolutely sound one.

But his tactics lacked a well-thought through Alinsky-ite plan. Governor Blagojevich simply refused to meet Reverend Meeks while the kids were not in school and the boycott failed. In frustration and perhaps with serious intent, Reverend Meeks has threatened to run against Governor Blagojevich should he seek re-election.

There is no doubt that Reverend Meeks has a strong

base. He has grown his Salem Baptist Church into a powerful community and political organisation. Salem's meeting place, the House of Hope, is not so much a church as a cross between a freight distribution warehouse and a music arena. In fact, it does host pop concerts (though it does not serve any function as a distribution warehouse). Located in Pullman, just north of Riverdale, on the Bishop Ford Freeway, unless you are very attentive you would not distinguish the House of Hope from the spattering of industrial and distribution facilities that lie both sides of you. The church is reputed to have around 25,000 members with 6,000 to 7,000 attending each Sunday. And on any such Sunday you are likely to be sitting with local politicians of significance, such as Jesse Jackson Jr or Anthony Beale, as well as visiting politicians or even the odd R&B star such as R Kelly.

Its political power is significant. Reverend Jesse Jackson Sr has earmarked Reverend Meeks as a future leader of his black empowerment organisation, Rainbow Push. Salem has trained thousands of voter registration registrars, critical to the voter mobilisation effort.* Reverend Meeks made his name when he worked with Alderman Beale (who was not yet elected) on a campaign to get a referendum on the ballot in 1998 to close liquor stores in much of Roseland. The behaviourist instinct unites both Reverend Meeks and Anthony Beale. Continuing the behaviourist theme, Reverend Meeks reached

---

*Mick Dumke, *Chicago Reader*, January 26, 2007.

out to evangelical and other Christian leaders, during an abortive run on the Democratic nomination for the Governorship in 2006. Reverend Meeks' strong anti-gay and anti-abortion stances were seen as a potential coalition builder for him.*

All of this sits rather uneasily with the people of Altgeld Gardens who don't see the Meeks/Beale brand of moralistic, church-centred politics as relevant to them. Their problems are economic and social as well as about individual behaviour.

Whether you choose to join a gang, abuse drugs and alcohol, get a job, educate yourself, seek the health care you need, adopt a healthy diet, stick with the family or play around, the choices that determine personal, family and community destiny are all consequential. Unless the underlying issues are addressed also then the chances that the right choices will be made are diminished. In communities such as Altgeld Gardens those chances are radically reduced. It is not that there is no likelihood of success. It is just that the chances of success are so small that it almost inevitably leads to despair. It's easy to say, having never been in their situation, that the people of Altgeld Gardens should behave differently. But as one resident said to me, 'Your dreams will never be realised in Altgeld.'

There are many who have not given up on Altgeld Gardens. Paulette Edwards, who runs a family support group, Project 18, is typical of a never-say-die

---

*Sarah Pulliam, *Christianity Today*, November 4, 2006.

attitude that still exists there. She grew up in Altgeld Gardens and always felt an irresistible pull back to the area.

She says: 'My family always ask me why are you still here? Because my whole life I sat with my family and friends and we would say why don't those people do this for themselves? Why can't they do that? Get themselves sorted. But they can't that's why. So I decided to make a difference rather than just talking about it or moralising. To give back to the community which gave me so much.'

That is the tragedy of what has happened in Altgeld. It was so much better. Paulette describes a community that was thriving during the 1950s and 1960s. There was a can-do attitude amongst the residents. On a summer's night the sounds you'd hear would be those of a lively neighbourhood, neighbours were friends, everyone pitched in and kept everything neat. On a Friday night, young people would wander over to the Carver leisure hall for a dance.

Paulette Edwards describes the change: 'Altgeld Gardens used to be vibrant, now it's dilapidated. There's an old phrase in black communities, 'It takes a village.' That's the way it used to be here. Everyone looked after one another and looked after the kids in the neighbourhood. If a kid stepped out of line, their parents would be told about it instantly. Now the adults are frightened of the kids and things are out of control.'

Loretta Augustine Herron who was a community activist in the 1980s and features in *Dreams from My*

Father as the character 'Angela' has a similar perspective. She is now a teacher and lives in Calumet City.

'I ran the Girl Guides there for thirteen years. We took trips. We had fundraisers, sold cookies and the like. And for thirteen years we took girls and their families to Florida. They went to Disney, Epcot. Everything. It was so valuable.'

'I remember when I was a little girl looking at a picture of the wind tunnel at Niagara Falls in a school book but all the kids in the picture were white. I was so desperate for those girls in Altgeld Gardens to have the opportunities that those white kids had and I like to think that's what we did.'

Later on, after she became a teacher, she realised that Altgeld Gardens was becoming more self-contained, more insular.

'One time I took a group of kids from Carver Middle School to Brookfield Zoo. Brookfield was out of town and it's got more to it than Lincoln Park Zoo. On the way, one of the kids piped up and said, 'Wow, what are those tall buildings over there?' Then I realised that one or two of the kids had never been downtown before and didn't know what it looked like.

'Then some of the other kids said to him, 'Why don't you come to the lake with us one day? The kid responded, 'Chicago has a lake?' Now that's not typical but the fact was that there was a kid who hadn't been out of Altgeld Gardens or maybe Roseland at a stretch is unbelievable. The horizon of many people in Altgeld is Altgeld and that is just so limited.'

The limited horizon of Altgeld Gardens is echoed by Paulette Edwards: 'I am so worried that we are throwing away the legacy of Martin Luther King. *Brown v Board of Education, Topeka*, the civil rights struggles, were in part about self-improvement. That was a key message. Many of the kids do not know about those struggles.

'The kids are at Carver Elementary School, and were at Carver Middle School before it closed this summer. But they don't know who George Washington Carver was.

'We came through that era so we could get an education, get a job, and that is going. Most of these families can't afford to go to the baseball, to a play or to a movie. They never go downtown because they can't afford anything there. It just lifts the lids off their kids' expectations and they know that that world isn't something they can give to their kids so they stay away. Besides, it is an $8 round trip so they just can't afford it.'

Actually, the civil rights movement had begun to create opportunities in the neighbourhood by the end of the 1960s. Under pressure, Mayor Richard J. Daley had established a community organisation called the Urban Progress Center (UPC) in neighbourhoods such as Altgeld Gardens.

Essentially, UPC assessors would visit families, evaluate what their needs were and ensure that available public services were geared towards those needs. They would also provide the service itself. This funnelling of support could include everything from food parcels, to education needs, mental health services, job brokerage or college advice. Many of the assessors were residents of Altgeld Gardens itself and that was critical to service provision. Paulette Edwards' mother was one of those who became an assessor. A friend of Paulette's also managed to get a job with the American Medical Association where she is still working forty years later through the UPC.

Then the funding for the UPC was cut. The model of active welfare had worked, and then it was gone. It has been replaced with a welfare of sorts but it is passive welfare. The Family Works service is a tick box exercise. You go along, fill in a questionnaire about your employment or skills needs then you go into the filing system, resurfacing only rarely. If you are lucky, you might get a food parcel. In reality, this is Family Works' basic utility.

As Linda Randle says of the cutting of UPC, 'Mayor [Richard J.] Daley would do good stuff for a while when the pressure was on but then after a while he would cut the funding and move it elsewhere to appease another group.'

There is local community website, *www.altgeldgardens.com*, which has a visitor board for people to post messages. Reading through the archive of messages is fascinating. Two things immediately become apparent when reading them. Firstly, the warm memories that people have of the area. Secondly, that few of them still live in Altgeld Gardens and seem to be talking about a community that once existed, could exist again, but for now is locked in a collective memory.

Makeyah Miller, now living in New Orleans, wrote on the website:

'Yes, I'm a product of Altgeld Gardens, and honey you don't have to beg my pardon, for I'm not ashamed of the mighty 'AG', because there a solid foundation was laid for me. It was called a housing project, however, we didn't see; for we lived together as one big family. Garden spot of America it was named, and in the sixties it was noted for fame ... People lived well, poverty we did not see, a working parent always supported the family. Roller skating at the Catholic and Children's Building too, gave us productive recreation to do!

'What is Altgeld like today? Who can say? Are the people willing to grow? Do you know? Is there a desire to restore a once wonderful community as before? Can it blossom again in our society? Yes, if contributions are made by you and me!'*

Once again, the theme is clear. A once-thriving community, round about the time of the late 1960s it takes a sharp turn for the worse. What happened?

Established originally as a transitional community, based on low rents to enable people to save for their first home, Altgeld Gardens had managed to sustain a balance in the early years following its construction in 1945, despite the flow of families in and out. Its residents were by and large the families of African-American servicemen who had given their service in World War II. To have expected them to return to 'coldwater' slums

---

*http://www.altgeldgardens.com/id68.html

that did not even have hot water was not a just response to their service.

In the late 1960s, under the direction of the US Department for Housing and Urban Development (HUD), stricter conditions were applied to rents in the area. Suddenly they were up to a third of a person's salary. As a result, many of the more affluent and, frankly, more aspirational families moved out of the area. If you are going to pay a rent that could secure you a house in a more affluent part of town then why not move there? One of the main reasons to stay in Altgeld Gardens was removed. Families that were already struggling were the ones that were left behind.

An unforeseen consequence of the change in rental policy was that Altgeld Gardens was shifting away from a balanced community towards one that was increasingly dependent on welfare. The shift would occur over a decade or more but it was perceptible. It was certainly understood locally and this was a further disincentive for more affluent families to remain as the community was starting to deteriorate. Public housing provision had come to be seen as a safety net. The problem with safety nets is that unless they are so taut that a person bounces up off them, they can engulf whole communities. In practice, an increasing proportion of Altgeld Gardens' families were dependent and they were stranded in the area, unable to leave.

It was just the sort of community that was a sitting duck for gang activity. From the 1970s onwards, the gangs moved in and they slowly took control of the entire community. American welfare is miserly. In fact, it is largely dispensed in the form of food stamps. Rent for those on welfare in Altgeld is cheap, just $90 a month or so. Even so, if you are unemployed and have been for a while (cash benefits are time-limited in the US which is tough especially on unmarried mothers), that is not an easy bill to pay. In reality, if you can't get a job or you are unable to work and have no income, there are only two ways to pay the bill. You can sell your food stamps at a discount which means your family goes hungry or malnourished. Or you can earn your income illegally by becoming involved in the drugs trade.

In American popular culture it is common to see drugs being distributed on the street corner. In Altgeld Gardens, they are distributed by the dumpsters, groups of kids huddled by trash handing out trash. Originally, there were two gangs operating in Altgeld, the Black Gangster Disciples (the 'BDs') and the Black P. Stone Nation (the 'Stones.') There are now up to five gangs operating in the area with the Vice Lords, Four Corner Hustlers and Gangster Disciples making up a nefarious oligopoly.

It is difficult to get an accurate figure of how extensive drug use is but a reasonable estimate seems to be that anything between a third and 40 percent of residents are drug-dependent. There is an equal split between heroin and crack cocaine, with the former gaining in popularity. Dealers will take over houses for a period of time to coordinate the operation and hoard the product in exchange for meeting the rent of the house. Everyone knows where these houses are but nothing seems to be done about it. Why risk your personal safety by informing the police, especially if nothing is going to be done?

Where there are drugs there are guns. Residents talk of a time in the early nineties when it seemed there was a murder a week in Altgeld Gardens. A police station was opened and things seemed to calm down for a while. It has now closed again as of 2003. The day before I arrived, there had been a shooting and an eerie silence enveloped the place. A 14-year-old boy had shot a 19-year-old girl. The week before there had been another shooting. In the last quarter of 2007, there were 11 shootings that resulted in death in Altgeld Gardens. Kids as young as eleven years old have access to guns.

Linda Randle was forever fearful for the safety of her grandchildren. She said: 'My grand-kids used to want to play at the basketball ring but I would stop them because there were young kids there with guns. The irony is that the basketball ring was put there to distract people from the gangs.

'The people themselves bear some responsibility. They just accept it. They know their kids have guns but they don't stop it. They cover up for one another. It's false loyalty as well as distrust of the police.

'There was this guy I used to buy from, a door-to-door salesman. He got beaten up for his money one night. He told me who did it so I confronted them. They said they would sort it out and not to call the police. But they did nothing.'

With the social changes, including the arrival of people from other housing projects that are being demolished, there is suddenly a wave of gang activity once again. As a local resident, Kim, says: 'It used to be that the "Stones" would control this block and the "BDs" would control that block but now they are all mixed in together since the rehab and that's created issues. We are told that people should learn to get along. And they will. By killing each other.'

Of course, as also accompanies gang activity, many of the residents are ex-felons and it is very difficult for them to secure employment. In fact, the ex-felon employment agency is in downtown Chicago so it is difficult for them to get there. Recently, the Chicago Housing Authority attempted to mandate that everyone who lived in public housing should work a minimum of twenty-five hours per week. The hard reality is that drug-users can't pass drug tests, ex-felons can't get jobs, so the mandate was quietly forgotten. Altgeld Gardens' social problems cannot be solved by the wave of a legislative magic wand.

The change in the social structure of Altgeld Gardens and the arrival of the gangs was bad enough for the community. However, in the late 1970s and early 1980s an economic hurricane was about to hit and that was the most significant change in the life chances of local residents.

A significant proportion of Altgeld Gardens residents relied on the local steel mills for employment. Proud firms such as US Steel, LTB Steel and Wisconsin

Steel were all located in close proximity to Altgeld Gardens and these were the economic engine of the neighbourhood. There are no offices nearby, no retail in the neighbourhood apart from a dingy little shop supplying liquor, candy, soda, potato chips and little else (though it does stock one item of clothing for sale: a single Obama '08 T-shirt). The steel mills then were essential to the well being of Altgeld Gardens from one generation to the next.

Already sliding down a slippery slope, the community was suddenly propelled over the precipice. Now estimates suggest that anything up to 80 percent of Altgeld Gardens' residents are workless. Even those who are able to hold down a steady job find the environment almost impossible to raise a family properly. In a community with poverty and low achievement, family breakdown, dearth of aspiration, problems with drugs and crime, and poor schooling, the chances for a child to succeed are small.

Kids in Altgeld Gardens make good progress in the early years and programmes such as Project 18 help to engage both the parents and the kids in education. By the 8th grade (13 years old), 51 percent of kids are still not at 6th grade standard. What is worse is that there is evidence that more of them had been at 6th grade standard in 6th grade than are now at that standard in 8th grade. They are slipping. Many of them are already leading adult lives by that age. That can't help.

Linda Randle described the situation a friend of hers was facing: 'There are good families in Altgeld but they tend to get out or get sucked into the despair of the place. I know one guy who has a good, steady job. He is a postal worker. All four of his kids are on drugs. It's an incredibly tough place.'

Paulette Edwards says: 'The whole theory of *No Child Left Behind* means that kids have to improve their attainment levels so that no child is left behind. They've had to drop that because if they rigidly enforced it then it could be a case of most children left behind.'

There is always hope. Paulette Edwards finds green shoots of optimism that she wants to grow.

She says: 'There is this heartbreaking story about a little boy whose mother was on drugs and he decided to support his family. He started travelling to The Loop everyday to sell candy and basically whatever he could get his hands on. He is a real entrepreneur. What a story! How much potential does that kid have? I'm desperate to find him and get my hands on him. So much potential! I am determined to get one kid, just one kid, all the way through. Then it is all worth it.'

Linda Randle knows the boy and it appears that he has expanded his enterprise. She said, 'There are now five boys that go to The Loop to sell candy everyday. I hear that they are quite accomplished.'

What a success it would be to get just one through. It would be a triumph to get five through. It was with this spirit that Barack Obama arrived in the neighbourhood.

❧

Working with people such as Linda Randle, Barack Obama organised his most successful campaign in Altgeld Gardens, though he would not be there to see its full success. A resident he called 'Sadie' pointed out an ad soliciting bids to remove asbestos from the Altgeld Gardens Management Office. It is not completely clear whether Obama was passing the credit to 'Sadie' or he had spotted it himself or, as seems possible, it was pointed out to him by Linda Randle, who was already working on the issue at the Ida B. Wells Project.

'Sadie' was determined to intervene and a meeting was arranged at the CHA office downtown. They were fobbed off with a denial that there was asbestos anywhere other than in the Management offices. Fortunately, 'Sadie' was too shrewd to be appeased so easily and she insisted on seeing proof that the homes had been tested for asbestos. The report was promised but it never showed up. So the residents got together to go back to the CHA offices and protest and insist that the CHA director attend a public meeting in Altgeld.

Eight of the residents went downtown and when they arrived, TV cameras were there to greet the small but determined group. When the deputy director of the CHA saw the cameras she then agreed to a meeting on the issue with the residents and also admitted that no tests had been done on their homes to see if any of the construction was done with asbestos. A meeting with her boss was arranged in Altgeld Gardens.

At the Altgeld meeting with the CHA director, chaos ensued in front of the TV cameras. Perhaps everyone was so excited at the presence of the director that they were desperate to offload their frustrations and needs.

'Sadie' lost heart and it seems that Obama did also, frustrated at the inertia of the system. During this episode, Barack Obama had confided his sense of powerlessness to his future colleague, Johnnie Owens.

Owens said: 'Barack basically talked about how tough it was to generate real results through organising and that it was embarrassing to him to have the residents out of control.' Jerry Kellman has quoted Barack Obama as saying: 'We are not making large-scale change and I want to be involved in doing that.'*

Despite their down-heartedness, the campaign had actually achieved a considerable amount. Asbestos was tested for, adding force to any future argument about the need to rehabilitate Altgeld Gardens, enough noise had been created to get the local politicians interested and, ultimately, there was a commitment to get some investment into the neighbourhood.

Barack Obama underestimates the legacy that he left in Altgeld Gardens. He had a tough job there but he gave the residents the self-confidence to carry on without him. Loretta Augustine Herron, 'Angela', speaks most positively about the impact that Barack Obama had upon her and the local communities in Roseland.

She said: 'Organising is so valuable to me. My becoming a teacher has such a lot to do with Barack Obama.'

'I'm not the only one who Barack empowered. He

---

*Serge Kovaleski, *The New York Times*, July 7, 2008.

made me understand who I was and my self worth. You know what? I've done it.

'He trained hundreds of us across the whole of the South Side and he increased the DCP organisation by adding more churches. Ten churches became twenty-two under Barack and different denominations not just Catholic. Don't forget churches come with communities and neighbourhoods.

'He was tireless in his devotion to the cause and was incredibly hard-working. He would work seven days a week, sometimes from 7.30 a.m. until after ten at night. But his best accomplishment was training us and empowering us. It is a gift that keeps on giving. His legacy is still there. It is immeasurable.

'He was deeply affected by his experience on the South Side of Chicago. But he kind of worked out how things worked. He knew that you can only affect real change through the power of government.'

'There was something he used to say to me that I will always cherish. 'Stay to the high road' and it will be OK. Stay to the high road.'

Or to put it more bluntly, as another Altgeld Gardens resident, Gail, said: 'He's no phoney. He for real.'

And as the 2008 election approached, Paulette Edwards and a few members of the community pulled together to initiate a voter registration drive. They sat with an elderly member of the Altgeld Gardens community, a 72 year-old man, the same age as Barack Obama's opponent John McCain. He wasn't registered to vote. In fact, he had never been registered. At first, he met the volunteers with embarrassed silence. The reason he had never registered to vote? He couldn't read or write and he had kept that secret for most of his life because he was ashamed. Now he confessed and a weight was lifted off. He picked up the pen and the volunteers helped him to register. He had finally opened up for one simple reason. This time he couldn't miss out. This time he was going to vote. He was going to vote for Barack Obama. And he was able to finally be honest about what had held him back for his entire life.

4

Harold Washington

*'It's not a case of black or white. We need someone who
will do things right. Bye, bye, blackbird. Your record,
Bernie, shows you are tough. And as for us, we have
been pushed enough. Bye, bye, blackbird.'*
Campaign song for the Bernie Epton for Mayor Campaign 1983.*

SAT IN PEARL'S PLACE, ON the intersection of East Per-
shing Road and South Michigan Avenue, in Bronzeville
on Chicago's South Side, Al Kindle explains the bond
between Harold Washington and Barack Obama. Pearl's
Place is a traditional diner specialising in Deep South
home cooking, where you sit surrounded by portraits of
African-American stars of screen and stage, the likes of
Ella Fitzgerald, Sam Cooke and Sammy Davis Jr.

Al Kindle was Harold Washington's 2nd Ward coor-
dinator in 1983, ran Barack Obama's campaign in Lake

---

*Dempsey J. Travis, *Harold Washington: The People's Mayor*, p. 190.

County, Indiana, and was Obama's 'street heat' (i.e. on the ground man) in his Senate race. Accordingly, he has had a birds-eye view of Chicago politics for over three decades. In the 2004 campaign alone, he recruited 6,000–7,000 volunteers and distributed 1.5 million pieces of literature for Obama.

He has been a political activist since the 1970s and can see the connections that exist from Martin Luther King through Harold Washington and Jesse Jackson Sr and now to Barack Obama. Just in case anyone was under the impression that Obama has come from nowhere, it turns out that he sits astride a formidable, independent political organisation that was established as a response to segregation and African-American deprivation in Chicago. These political activists are central to understanding how America has travelled from the civil rights movement to Barack Obama's movement for change. It was a political strategy that was incubated in Chicago but has now gone national.

One eye on his email, using his mobile as a paddle to keep a number of political ping-pong balls in play, and working his way through a plate of deep-fried catfish and grits, Al Kindle explains exactly how a political strategy was developed from the 1970s onwards.

African-Americans in Chicago had a formidable challenge in the 1970s. They made up just over a third of the city's population so while they were a sizeable minority, they had insufficient numbers to stop them from being locked outside of the fifth floor in City Hall. At least that was the case until Harold Washington spectacularly seized power in 1983 and became the city's first black Mayor. That campaign contained the seeds of the political strategy that was to enable Barack Obama to become the first black presidential candidate in US history.

Al Kindle explains: 'We were trying to persuade Harold Washington to run back in 1982. There had long been discussions about how we could get a black Mayor in Chicago. Some of the groundwork had been done but we went for it in 1982.'

'Harold said to us, 'I'll only do it if you register 150,000 new voters.' So we went away and worked on that. We got him 250,000 new voters so he ran. We had to get 85 percent to 90 percent of these voters to vote and over 85 percent of them had to vote for Harold. That's exactly what happened. There was a dream split in the anti-Harold vote between the then Mayor Jane Byrne and Richard M. Daley.'

Harold Washington won the Democratic nomination with just 36 percent of the vote. That he won at all was miraculous and testament to astounding political organisation.

Al Kindle continues, 'We know how to play the rules in Chicago. We understand hanging chads and all the rest of it! We understand the rules and change them for our benefit. Jesse Jackson's presidential runs in 1984 and 1988 also prepared the ground for Obama. The rule changes in the Democratic nomination process as a result of that gave Obama the opportunity to win.

'What we did for Barack in Iowa is exactly the same as we did for Harold and as we did for Obama's run for

US Senate. We played the rules, registered the voters and built a coalition.

'There are critical differences between Barack and Harold Washington of course. Washington was more tied to his base whereas Barack Obama can not afford to appeal to only one constituency.'

Underlying this political organisation that has spanned four decades was a singular set of objectives. The main purpose was to get black leaders into office so that they could build confidence in the ability of African-Americans to govern. It was not about reparations or retribution or compensation or anything else that could exacerbate Chicago or America's racial separation. It was far more pragmatic than that. It was about governance.

This pragmatism is what drives people like Al Kindle who have been involved in this political struggle for a long time.

He says, 'It is about a symbolic shot. A President Obama will address a number of structural issues. Once someone has made it, it changes the game. Obama can't have and doesn't have a black-only agenda. But if he governs wisely then that changes the whole thing. That's what it's about, governance. If he governs wisely then that will change things for all of us.'

This is a view shared across Chicago's South Side. In Altgeld Gardens, person after person said that their expectations of an Obama presidency were pragmatic. They simply wanted him to be 'a good President' or 'govern wisely.'

To understand the umbilical cord that links Barack Obama to Harold Washington to Jesse Jackson Sr to

Martin Luther King, it is necessary to look at the history behind Harold Washington and how some of the elements allowing an African-American candidate to have a realistic shot at the White House were already in place. That history is the prologue to the Barack Obama story. It is there that the seemingly impossible became reality. It was in that political organisation that the next stage of the civil rights movement gestated.

⋙

George Clinton's funk band, Parliament, described the change in the racial profile of America's cities in 1970s as one of 'vanilla suburbs' and 'chocolate cities'. The song 'Chocolate City' was mainly referring to Washington, DC but a similar, though not quite as spectacular, process was also occurring in Chicago.

By 1980, 'white flight' had increased Chicago's African-American population to 40 percent, the white population having declined from 60 to 47.6 percent. Alongside this, income was falling in the city. It fell by 6.6 percent between 1979 and 1985 while nationally it had increased by 3.7 percent in the same period. Between 1970 and 1980 median income for Chicago's black population fell from 77 percent to 68 percent of white income in the same period.*

---

*Pierre Clavel and Wim Wiewel, *Harold Washington and the Neighbourhoods: Progressive City Government in Chicago, 1983–1987,* p. 22.

The economic consequences of segregation were becoming absolutely clear. Mayor Richard J. Daley left Chicago with a number of inheritances. An intensely segregated city with minority communities concentrated in public housing projects (comprising the poor neighbourhoods along South State Street on the South Side and communities in the West Side also), was one of the most lasting consequences of the underlying principles guiding his tenure. It left those communities as sitting ducks when the ill winds of economic change arrived. And in the 1970s and 80s they did.

Mayor Richard J. Daley was a student of power above all else. He inherited, though he would smart at the description, a political machine that had originally been built by Mayor Anthon Cermak (who at a political rally in 1933 had been hit by a bullet meant for President Franklin Delano Roosevelt). The maintenance of that machine was conducted through an extensive system of political patronage that, in almost Chinese Communist Party style or perhaps Ba'athist Iraq, blended political organisation and public administration. If you wanted a municipal job you had to do your groundwork in servicing the machine in your precinct or neighbourhood, distributing Daley campaigning literature, herding voters into the polling place, fundraising, selling tickets to Daley dinners and a myriad of other activities designed to sustain Richard J. Daley in office.

When Jesse Jackson Sr arrived in Chicago from North Carolina, he went to see Mayor Daley about the possibility of getting a job through City Hall. He was told, much to his vexation, that he should go and see his local ward committeeman and if he did some political work there might be a low level city job for him further down the line.* The machine was run through the Cook County Democratic Party of which Richard J. Daley was chairman. Eventually, the system unravelled following the 1979 Shakman ruling which decreed that, other than for a few exceptional positions, it was illegal for any political factors to be taken into account in the recruitment of public employees. Without patronage, the system broke down but that was only after Mayor Daley's time. While he was in office it was very much in operation and it seemed insurmountable.

As Mayor Daley is often quoted as saying, 'Good politics was good government' and that applied to the city's race relations also. His strategy was to concentrate the black vote in a few wards on the South Side. This made political sense: it would be more difficult for his ascendancy to be challenged if there was a ceiling on the number of aldermen that the black community could influence. It also, from his perspective, made for good government, avoiding flashpoints such as that in 1963 when a civil rights activist, John Walsh, bought a property on Mayor Daley's street and moved in two black students.

The response of the local community was to send hate messages to the students and throw rocks through the windows. When police entered the apartment they

---

*Mike Royko, *Boss: Richard J. Daley of Chicago*, p .26.

spread excrement on the walls. The real estate agent who managed the move was instructed by the 11th Ward Democratic Organisation that the students were no longer living there and that white residents must be moved in. Given that the City of Chicago controlled real estate licenses, the agent complied.*

The irony is that it was the black vote that, certainly in the early years, had sustained Mayor Daley in office. In 1963, he actually lost the white vote to his political rival (and former mentor) Benjamin Adamowski who was now a Republican. But a huge black vote gave him a winning margin of 138,000. As Mike Royko wrote: 'The people who were trapped in the ghetto slums and the nightmarish public housing projects, the people who had the worst school system and were most often degraded by the Police Department, the people who were ignored as part of the campaign trail, had given him his third term. They had done it quietly, asking for nothing in return. Exactly what they got.'† Daley's huge success in winning the black vote was through the operation of a sub-machine run by Congressman William Dawson.‡ That delivered an almost 90 percent vote for him. With the death of Dawson in 1970, the sub-machine would crumble and there would begin to be a realignment of the black vote in Chicago based on a more rational and hard-headed assessment of collective and self-interest.

---

*Mike Royko, pp. 134–136.

†Mike Royko, p .132.

‡David Bernstein, *Chicago Magazine*, September 2008.

Already, by the end of the 1960s, the black vote was starting to bleed away from the Democrats. In 1968, in the aftermath of race riots in the city that had left eleven people dead and five hundred injured following the assassination of Martin Luther King, turnout amongst black voters collapsed. Republican Richard Ogilvie won the gubernatorial election of that year, partly as a result of a dozen predominantly black wards that had produced 341,000 votes to the Democrats in 1964, only delivering 243,000 in 1968.*

In 1971, Mayor Daley was re-elected against the Republican candidate, Richard Friedman. In assembling a coalition of liberals, independents and disgruntled blacks, Friedman had tried to overturn the Daley machine. He only secured 29 percent of the vote to which one person said: 'This proves that if you put together a coalition of independents, blacks, liberals and Republicans, there is no way Daley can keep you from getting twenty-nine percent of the vote.'†

That was true. However, sometimes large defeats mask some underlying forces that can come together further down the line to claim victory for a seemingly marginal coalition. The Barry Goldwater purist conservative coalition in 1964 was developed and extended by Nixon, Reagan and then the two Bush Presidents. The coalition that was spectacularly defeated in 1971 in Chicago hinted at an independent coalition that could

*Mike Royko, p. 195.
†Mike Royko, p. 215.

put a non-Daley machine candidate into office. A better candidate would be needed. They would have to run under the Democratic banner rather than the Republican. The African-American vote would have to be registered and turn out en masse. The Latino vote would have to be tempted into the coalition.

If all these conditions were met and an organisation was created to mobilise the coalition, it was conceivable that a politician independent of Mayor Richard J. Daley could win. The African-American vote when combined with Hyde Park liberals, independents and the Latino vote was a viable coalition and the hopes of the disempowered and dispossessed communities in Chicago rested on it being converted from concept to power. With the right candidate that could happen. Such a candidate was available: Harold Washington.

᠅

When Barack Obama was teaching in the University of Chicago Law School, on his office wall was a picture of Harold Washington standing by the Chicago lakeside.* Through his frustrations and tribulations in Altgeld Gardens, Barack Obama had a constant emotional, philosophical and, as in the asbestos campaign, practical engagement with the administration of the terrifically charismatic Mayor Harold Washington.

---

*The image can be seen at *http://www.nytimes.com/imagepages/2008/05/11/us/11chicago_CA3ready.html*.

Just as his work organising local communities was his first real experience of trying to change lives through the mobilisation of power, the Chicago of the mid-1980s was his first view of what could be done with greater resources of political power at your disposal. The early death of Mayor Washington in 1987 left more questions than answers both for expectant Chicago communities and for Barack Obama personally. David Mendell, Barack Obama's biographer, considers that the example of Harold Washington must have demonstrated what could have been achieved with real political power in a way that could not be achieved through year after year of community organising. Perhaps that was so but looking at Harold Washington's time could just as easily impart the lesson that even with the power of City Hall at your disposal, change was incremental, won through conflict as much as consensus, and takes time to impact everyday lives. Washington achieved much but it was not without struggle.

Barack Obama reacted, like countless others on Chicago's South Side, in a deeply personal way to the death of Washington on November 25, 1987. Obama was already perturbed by his own perceived lack of progress in improving the communities that he served. By the following September he was at Harvard Law School investing in a different future for himself.

Jerry Kellman would constantly encourage Barack Obama to move on and to be realistic about his chances of making a real difference in Altgeld Gardens. He would regularly caution Obama: 'Life is short Barack.

If you're not trying to really change things out here, you might as well forget it.'* It could be easy to understand how and why Barack Obama would get frustrated. He despaired at characters such as the pastor of the local church in Altgeld Gardens. Whenever he would suggest that the community organise to try to get a better deal from the CHA, 'Reverend Johnson' would push back. 'CHA ain't the problem. Problem is these young girls out here, engaging in all manner of fornication.'† It would seem that the behaviourist perspective was just as strong in Barack Obama's day as it is today.

There was little doubt that Harold Washington was improving things but Barack Obama was impatient to see change occur more rapidly. Following a civic opening ceremony by Mayor Washington, Barack Obama was frustrated that the community activists whom he took down there weren't able to secure a commitment to get the Mayor to come to a rally that he was organising later that year. His colleague Will said to Barack Obama at this time, 'I think you're just trying to do a good job. But I also think you ain't never satisfied. You want everything to happen fast. Like you got something to prove out here.'‡

Obama concedes that he felt that he did have something to prove – to the people of Altgeld, to Kellman, to his late father, to himself. Will had a slightly different

---

*Barack Obama, *Dreams from My Father*, p. 229.
†Barack Obama, p. 229.
‡Barack Obama, p. 226.

take on it, seeing it as a bit of jealousy at Harold Washington. He said, 'See, you like the young rooster, Barack, and Harold's like the old rooster. Old rooster came in, and the hens gave him all the attention. Made the young rooster realise he's got a thing or two to learn.'* At a certain point Obama wondered whether Harold Washington shared his sense that he was a prisoner of fate.

Then came disaster. As Barack Obama wrote, 'Harold didn't pay ... critics much attention. He saw no reason to take any big risks, no reason to hurry. He said he'd be mayor for the next twenty years. And then death: sudden, simple, final, almost ridiculous in its ordinariness, the heart of an overweight man giving way.'†

Mayor Harold Washington's death left a community shell-shocked, people in despair, and the bitter taste of hope denied. His legacy, both in spirit and in practice, still shrouds Chicago today. Around him were people well versed in the art of political power. The lessons they learned in getting a black mayor elected are the lessons that were re-applied to get the first black candidate nominated for a run at the presidency. Barack Obama owes an immense amount to Harold Washington and the people who got him elected.

❧

Upon his victory in the mayoral election on April 12,

---

*Barack Obama, p. 230.

†Barack Obama, p. 287.

1983, Harold Washington declared, 'Blacks, whites, Hispanics, Jews, gentiles, Protestants and Catholics have joined to form a new Democratic coalition and to begin in this place a new Democratic movement.'* That is precisely what Harold Washington and the people who had organised for him and persuaded him to stand had achieved. Along with 80 percent of the black vote, Washington secured 65 percent of the Latino vote and 17 percent of his winning coalition was white, including a good chunk of the 'Lakeside liberals' and a number of poorer white voters. The movement had defeated the machine and Harold Washington was quick to declare: 'The machine, as we know it, is dead.'†

Two insults to Chicago's African-American community had made a run on the mayoralty inevitable in 1983. The next in line to be Mayor upon an existing incumbent's death was the president pro tem of the City Council. Upon the death of Mayor Richard J. Daley in December 1976, that was the black alderman Wilson Frost of the 34th Ward. However, when Alderman Frost arrived to enter the Mayor's office in City Hall he was prevented, at gunpoint by the Chicago Police Department, from entering. The power broker was a segregationist, a Democrat of Croatian descent. Tough 'Fast Eddie' Vrdolyak, who was eventually to end up as a

*Dempsey J. Travis, p. 195.

†Doug Gills, in Pierre Clavel and Wim Wiewel, *Harold Washington and the Neighbourhoods: Progressive City Government in Chicago, 1983–1987,* pp. 53–54.

Republican a decade or so later and was indicted by a Grand Jury in 2007 for fraud amongst other things, was refusing the support of his faction for Wilson Frost.

A huge demonstration ensued at City Hall. Little did they know that while Jesse Jackson Sr, founder of Operation PUSH, had received assurances from Wilson Frost that Frost was going to insist that he assume the position of Mayor, the reality was, in fact, very different. Wilson Frost did a deal with Eddie Vrdolyak to allow Michael Bilandic to become Mayor with Frost becoming chair of the Finance Committee. The deal was an embarrassment, betrayal and insult to Chicago's African-Americans when the mayoralty was theirs by constitutional right.

At the next mayoral election in 1979, Mayor Jane Byrne was able to defeat Michael Bilandic on the back of a coalition not dissimilar to that which was to elect Harold Washington in 1983. The purpose of the coalition was to gain more clout for the neighbourhoods instead of downtown Chicago and the airport alone.* Jane Byrne, instead of implementing the neighbourhood approach, did precisely the opposite, adding further insult to Chicago's black communities.

There is an important point here. This coalition was not just demographic but it had a substantive element. It was about *power* but was also about *public policy*. It was not just about proving that power could be won, it was about delivering an agenda. Many of the people

---

*Doug Gills, p. 50.

who were involved in this public policy development were also those who moved to centre-stage in achieving Harold Washington's victory. It included a number of refugees from the civil rights movement such as Dorothy Tillman, Anna Langford and Bobby Rush amongst others.*

So when Mayor Jane Byrne topped her refusal to increase employment for ethnic minorities in city jobs with the publication of a plan to focus development downtown, disregarding neighbourhoods such as Chinatown and Pilsen, she would inevitably face a strong challenge from the same coalition that had secured office for her in 1979. In protest at her policies, a boycott of Mayor Byrne's Chicago Fest in the summer of 1982 was organised by Jesse Jackson Sr. As a result, Stevie Wonder pulled out of the event much to the embarrassment of the Mayor.

At the core of the challenge was the massive voter registration drive. There were 300,000 unregistered black voters in Chicago and getting them on the register and into polling places was the fundamental building block of the campaign. It in turn worked as a movement rather than as an organisation, interlocking several different organisations, political figures and constituencies. This movement characteristic was crucial. Strongly driven forward by individuals such as Renault Robinson and Jesse Jackson Sr, the achievements of the voter registration campaign were phenomenal.

---

*Doug Gills, p. 44 and p. 51.

With the marketing expertise of the Soft Sheen hair products company combined with the organisational muscle of Operation PUSH and other organisations including the Chicago Black United Communities, the Citizens Committee, and the Chicago Urban League and others, the vast majority of those unregistered voters were registered.* Numbers vary but anything between 230,000 and 250,000 voters were registered by the time of the Mayoral election. Outside of this movement, groups such as the Illinois-Independent Precinct Organisation were also working to draft Harold Washington.† Backing from the churches, invoking the traditions of Martin Luther King, was secured, a final statement of support refined by none other than a Reverend Jeremiah Wright of the Trinity United Church of Christ who would later embarrass a member of his congregation, Barack Obama, in the presidential primary campaign of 2008.‡

Money came from a broad cross-section of the community but events where hundreds of small contributions were raised were a feature of the campaign. Reverend Jesse Jackson whipped an event at the Illinois pavilion into a frenzy of donation. On top of the major gifts received that night, at the end of the event the organisers noticed that the floor was covered with dollar bills and small change. They gathered it and counted

---

*Dempsey J. Travis, p. 149.

†Dempsey J. Travis, p. 151.

‡Dempsey J. Travis, p. 168.

over $40,000.* Everyone was contributing everything that they possibly could.

The end result of this phenomenal movement to elect Chicago's first black Mayor was victory in the Democratic primary for Harold Washington by only 30,000 votes over Mayor Jane Byrne, her vote having been split by the candidacy of Richard M. Daley, then State Attorney. Despite much of the Democratic vote fracturing along racial lines (with Vrdolyak, in particular, letting it be known none too discretely that he didn't wholeheartedly back the Democratic candidate), Harold Washington defeated the Republican candidate in the mayoral election itself, Bernie Epton, by just over 40,000 votes.

While a great many figures contributed to Harold Washington's victory, one in particular is worthy of note. Reverend Jesse Jackson is a figure who links what Reverend Martin Luther King was working towards in the 1960s with Barack Obama's presidential bid in 2008. With a slightly aggressive manner and egotistical reputation, it is easy to overlook the critical role of Jesse Jackson in the civil rights movement. It would be a grave mistake to do so.

As a close and demonstrative member of Martin Luther King's entourage, Jesse Jackson developed a reputation for organisation-building and practical achievement. Jackson had long been seeking to persuade King to move his operation north to Chicago and

---

*Dempsey J. Travis, p. 175.

this resulted in Jackson being tasked with establishing Operation Breadbasket, an off-shoot of King's SCLC, which was designed to arrange boycotts of business that were discriminatory in their commercial practices. He drew attention to himself for smearing the blood of the assassinated Martin Luther King on his jersey and appearing on television dressed in the same garment a day later.

Ultimately, he remained in Chicago to push Martin Luther King's agenda. When he fell out, irretrievably, with King's successor, Ralph Abernathy in 1971, forcing his ejection from the SCLC, Jackson established Operation PUSH which had some notable success in achieving economic concessions from businesses, including increasing minority employment and commercial contracts through boycotts of Coca-Cola, Anheuser Busch and Kentucky Fried Chicken.

In terms of politics it was in his ability to organise voter registration and mobilisation, following through on the spirit of Selma and the Voting Rights Act 1965, that Jesse Jackson has had the most impact. Through his own runs at the presidency in 1984 and 1988 he assembled the Rainbow Coalition which was designed to advance an agenda that included voting rights and social investment underpinned by voter registration and mobilisation. In practice, it meant that the Democratic Party was expanded by millions of young and African-American voters in the 1980s. It is this new base of voters recruited by Jesse Jackson that helped to make a successful run on the Democratic nomination possible for Barack Obama and, indeed, Senator Obama was endorsed by Jesse Jackson in March 2007.

That was not the only way in which the presidential bids of Jesse Jackson were of help to Barack Obama. In losing in 1988, but still with a strong block of support behind him, Jesse Jackson had the political clout to insist that the Democratic candidate Michael Dukakis agree to changes in the primary contest in exchange for Jesse Jackson's whole-hearted support. The deal was both to replace a winner-takes-all voting system and remove super-delegates (essentially, the Democratic Party great and good who account for 20% or so of the nomination votes). Though super-delegates were reinstated, the proportional system remained in place.

Tracking forward to 2008, the proportional system was an important element in allowing Barack Obama to remain competitive. It is difficult to see how he could have recovered from the Super Tuesday, February 5, 2008 results that included defeat in big states such as New York, New Jersey, Massachusetts and California, had a proportional voting system not been in place. The bloodline from Martin Luther King to Barack Obama is strong but Jesse Jackson is an arterial connection between the two.

The transmission wouldn't have been possible without Harold Washington. His administration succeeded in building on the work done by community organisations such as the Rehab Network to develop a strategy to shift City Hall's resources to the neighbourhoods. He adopted a more open style of administration, allowing greater dialogue and scrutiny, welcoming previously excluded voices and creating a more equitable distribution of City Hall's employment and contracting. South Side communities and others felt like they finally had a voice on their city's affairs and they did.

Washington was rewarded with a second term of office. In a further example of the continuity in the history of Chicago's politics, the victory was masterminded by a young political consultant who had joined Washington's administration as a media adviser. This was David Axelrod, now ensconced as Barack Obama's campaign supremo. His advice was to keep the campaign positive until the very end and defend Washington's record of achievement against the obstacles placed in his way by the 'Vrdolyak 29', a faction that was able to block Harold Washington for much of his first term.*

The campaign strategy was good enough for Washington to see off Jane Byrne again and win the election itself 54–40 over Eddie Vrdolyak, now running as an Independent under the 'Illinois Solidarity Party' label (he would end up as a Republican in much the same vein as politicians like Strom Thurmond who deserted the South Carolina Democrats following the Civil Rights Act in 1964).

It is difficult to overstate the importance of Harold Washington in the translation of the civil rights movement from the 1960s to the current day. The inspirational force of the man, the people around him, the

---

*Alton Miller, *Harold Washington: The Mayor, The Man*, p. 300.

tactics they deployed, the model of political organisation they innovated, all helped the transition of a movement into a credible campaign by an African-American, Barack Obama, in 2008. In some respects, it can be seen that the civil rights movement, dissipated and fragmented, had become urbanised following its fracture in the aftermath of the assassination of Martin Luther King. Its promise was again realised in Harold Washington's triumph.

Once again, the movement was not able to sustain itself independently of its figurehead. Harold Washington was chosen by the movement but once he accepted its plea, he then defined the movement. No one has taken his place in Chicagoan politics. Richard M. Daley, who won the election after Harold Washington's death, has succeeded in ensuring that no sustainable block of support has massed against his position as it did against Mayor Byrne. He has appointed a number of African-American aldermen who are in debt to him (in Chicago, aldermen are replaced by the Mayor when they do not complete their full term of office). Also, he has been more shrewd in meeting the needs of Chicago's disempowered communities than his father was.

Alderman Preckwinkle of the 4th Ward said this: 'Mayor Daley has done slightly better amongst the black community in election after election. We used to have strong candidates against him, people like Danny Davis and Bobby Rush. Running against him is so hopeless as his organisation is so strong and I guess there is an underlying satisfaction with him.'

The movement that Harold Washington left behind was ultimately to find another home a decade and a half later. Its new figurehead was to be Barack Obama and it moved to him finally in his campaign for US Senate in 2004. Of course, Illinois is different to Chicago, and the USA is different to Illinois, so it does not have the same form. The techniques, personalities and principles are there though. Most importantly, it is a movement and it is exceedingly politically powerful. It had to be to propel a young, one-term Senator from Illinois towards the White House.

Barack Obama is standing on the shoulders of giants and Harold Washington's shoulders are some of the broadest. As Al Kindle said, with a note of sorrow tinged with a hint of pride, 'I only wish Harold was here to see it.'

5

Obama's Rise

POLITICAL ADVANCEMENT is a fine art. A politician who has ambition needs to demonstrate their authenticity but also understand the pragmatic nature of the exercise. The theory is simple. Protect your base while simultaneously reaching out to new constituencies. In practice it is one of the most difficult endeavours to pull off imaginable.

Should you tilt too much towards your base then that is where you will stay. Reach out too far and you'll be left floating without anchor, a sell-out without purpose or meaning. This is not a cynical exercise or at least it need not be. At its very core politics is about power and how you exercise that power. It is about the end but it is also about the means. The challenge is to scoop the water from the lake without becoming enamoured by your own reflection, Narcissus-like. If you are truly motivated by your base, if you want to improve and change their lives, there is no point becoming introspective, you have to dip in. Therein lies the danger.

That is the very fundamental political task, to reach out but stay anchored. Now imagine that suddenly race is added to the mix and rather than a one-dimensional political task, suddenly you have to play two. The task becomes infinitely more complex. Now instead of leaning into the lake from the shore, you are dipping in with only two slippery rocks to stand on. It takes balance, poise and self-belief to get the water in the bucket. Only a politician of remarkable skill can meet such a challenge. Very few have succeeded without the inevitable accusations of sell-out or by staying on the rocks and failing to scoop the water. Barack Obama was game and determined to give it his best shot.

There is little doubt that following his legal training and tenure as president of the *Harvard Law Review* at Harvard Law School, Barack Obama returned to Chicago in 1991 with strong political ambitions. He registered 150,000 voters for the 1992 elections though Project Vote. Voter registration was a core component of all he was to achieve in politics further down the line. These voters would contribute towards the election of the first black woman to be elected for the Senate, Carol Moseley Braun. It was also a good place to meet key activists, political leaders, and, just as critically, donors who could finance nomination runs when the time came.

He was making the right political moves to build a network of people who had influence and came to know him. In 1993, he joined Davis, Miner, Barnhill & Galland, a civil rights firm with an independent ethos that distinguished it from other Richard M. Daley connected law firms. Its head was Judson Miner who had been Harold Washington's former counsel and founding member of the Chicago Council of Lawyers. Joining the firm was a political statement. It placed Barack Obama decidedly in the camp of the independents against the Daley machine.

Also, by living in Hyde Park, Barack Obama was defining himself as a liberal reformer, just like the Lakeside liberals who had coalesced around Harold Washington. These were independent, powerful and wealthy. Perhaps it is too much to calculate all of his early moves through the prism of political ambition. There is little doubt that the moves that he was making in his professional life both matched his instincts but would also prove to be politically advantageous further down the line.

Just prior to joining the law firm, Obama had married Michelle Robinson in the Trinity United Church of Christ. A formidable professional in her own right and someone who has become a dazzling presence on the national political scene, Michelle had taken the tough call of marrying someone with political ambitions. Their home life could never be anything close to conventional and at times they would have to endure long separations as Barack was first to spend most of the week in Springfield as State Senator and then in Washington as US Senator. Through this they managed to create some degree of normality. To see their home now in Hyde Park, barricaded and guarded, is a salutary lesson in how tough it is to combine family and political life. The strength of Michelle and Barack's relationship makes that combination a possibility where many others would fail.

Within three years of marriage, Obama would launch his first run for office. A State Senate seat, the 13th District, combining the Hyde Park neighbourhood, the University of Chicago and many of the poorer neighbourhoods of the South Side, was up for grabs. The sitting State Senator, Alice Palmer, was launching her own campaign for a Congressional seat, the 2nd District. Palmer backed Barack Obama as her successor, declaring to his announcement party in the lakefront Ramada Inn: 'In this room, Harold Washington announced for Mayor. Barack Obama carries on the tradition of independence in this district ... His candidacy is a passing of the torch.'*

However, Alice Palmer's campaign was not going particularly well and it became clear that she was going to lose to one of two strong candidates, Jesse Jackson Jr or the State Senate President, Emil Jones. She hoped that Obama would step aside and let her reclaim her State Senate seat. In the primary for the congressional seat, Palmer ended up with a derisory 10 percent. Obama not only refused but challenged Palmer's petitions to run which he alleged were filled with irregularities. He

---

*Ryan Lizza, *The New Yorker*, July 21, 2008.

was successful in having Alice Palmer's name removed from the ballot. He was on his way to Springfield.

It was there that Barack Obama learned how to be a politician. That is, he learned how to forge support for measures that would have a practical outcome and understood that this was a shifting process that needed constant attention and relationship building. After the State Senate became controlled by the Democrats in 2002, he was at his best. Obama did have an ability to reach across the aisle and forge bi-partisan consensus throughout his time in Springfield. That was a talent that was acknowledged by Republicans as well as Democrats. As Republican State Senator Kirk Dillard said in an ad for the Obama campaign, 'Obama worked on some of the deepest issues we had, and he was successful in a bipartisan way.'*

He was not very adept at building those political alliances at the beginning of his time in office. In fact, he had found it hard going, particularly with allies of Alice Palmer in Springfield. Slightly more experienced State Senators from Chicago, most particularly Rickey Hendon and Donne Trotter, were dismissive of him when he arrived in the state capital. Trotter labelled him as, 'a white man in a black face.'† During the passage of one of Obama's early bills in the Senate, an exchange on the Senate floor became confrontational and after the debate, almost bubbled over completely. Hendon had

---

*Eli Saslow, *Washington Post*, October 9, 2008.
†Eli Saslow.

launched into a mocking diatribe aimed at Obama, saying things such as 'I seem to remember a very lovely Senator by the name of Palmer – much easier to pronounce than Obama – and she always had cookies and nice things to say, and you don't have anything to give us around your desk. How do you expect to get votes?'*

Eventually, Obama built a strong alliance with Emil Jones, who became president of the Senate following the Democrats' victory in 2002, learned the art of the late night poker game with beers and cigars in building friendships, and toned down an aloof, academic manner, becoming a more artful politician in the process. His focus was on practical measures. During his time in the Illinois Senate he helped secure ethics and campaign finance reform, health-care improvements, increases in tax credits for less affluent families, increased subsidies for childcare, a whole raft of law and order measures targeting offenders who used date rape drugs, and some reforms to the police practice of racial profiling.

He once again locked horns with Hendon over this latter issue. Hendon had proposed a ban on racial targeting in conjunction with colleagues from the black caucus. His proposals were failing and then Barack Obama took up the cause. Obama moderated the provisions and got it passed with bipartisan support. Emil Jones was working to help Obama sponsor the right sort of legislation with a possible run for Congress, the Senate specifically, in mind. During the two years after the

_____
*Ryan Lizza.

Democrats were in the majority, Obama managed to sponsor 200 bills that became law and was the primary sponsor on over 20 measures. The one blot on his copybook was the fact that he had abstained from so many measures by voting 'present' 129 times. Though these votes were mainly tactical manoeuvres by the Democrats before they were in the majority, it was something that would cause Obama some difficulty later on in his political career.*

His performance was solid. Even by 1999, fours years into his time in Springfield, he felt confident enough to launch a bid for Congress. Obama decided to run against Congressman Bobby Rush who he felt had been weakened by an abortive attempt on City Hall the year before. How wrong he was.

Bobby Rush was one of those people in Chicago who had helped to extend the thread of the civil rights movement from Martin Luther King to Harold Washington and beyond. He had been involved with the SNCC, served as head of the Illinois Black Panther Party, and was an Alderman in which Harold Washington had invested his trust in the 1980s. The bid for Rush's seat is probably the one clearly identifiable mistake in Barack Obama's political career though ultimately he did manage to turn it to his medium-term advantage. It was a strange decision to run. The first poll Obama took in the campaign showed that Rush had a 90 percent to 10 percent lead over him with

---

*Eli Saslow.

his approval rating hitting just 8 percent.* During the campaign, Congressman Rush's son was shot outside his home. When the state legislature was called into a special session to vote on gun control laws, Obama was unable to return from holiday as a result of the illness of one of his daughters.

Bobby Rush told the *Chicago Tribune*, 'This vote was probably the most pivotal vote, one of the most important votes in memory before the General Assembly, and I just can't see any excuse that Mr Obama could use for missing this vote.'† Barack Obama lost the primary by a margin of two to one. At the hands of a skilled and self-confident politician, political defeats can be turned into opportunities. A weaker politician would have licked his wounds, gone back to Springfield and concentrated on what he had. For Barack Obama, this defeat was a springboard for something greater: a run at the US Senate. He told Emil Jones and a few others so and set about making it happen.

The race had given him a higher profile, critical for any future move on a congressional seat. It had given him a sense of the political coalition that could secure a nomination for him. His Senate seat was due to be re-districted. Obama ensured that his new district would not only include the communities in the South Side that were his voter base but also communities in The Loop, as this would give him access to liberal influencers,

---

*Barack Obama, *The Audacity of Hope*, p. 105.

†Quoted in David Mendell, *Obama: From Promise to Power*, p. 136.

the type of people who could finance a campaign for him.* If they became familiar with him, and he was their State Senator, that would help his chances. He now had a district with a localised balance of some of those groups of voters that have sustained his national campaign: African-American communities, white liberals and the college student vote. It also bore a striking similarity to the coalition that underpinned Harold Washington's two successful mayoral elections with the one exception that a significant Latino vote was not in that district.

The opportunity finally presented itself in 2003 when first-term Republican Senator Peter Fitzgerald announced that he was not going to run again. It is possible that Barack Obama would have looked to challenge him anyway but now that there was no incumbent to fight, the vacant Illinois Senator's seat drew a great deal of attention.

Obama would face two strong opponents for the nomination: Blair Hull, an independently wealthy stock investor, and Daniel Hynes, son of Tom Hynes. His father was a Richard J. Daley man who had been President of the State Senate and the powerful Cook County Assessor. Daniel Hynes had served as State Comptroller, where he had developed a good record and a statewide profile. Blair Hull had already got off to a flying start buying advertising slots as early as summer 2003.

The initial campaign strategy, with David Axelrod

---

*Ryan Lizza.

already calling the shots, had three basic elements. Firstly, Barack Obama had to get Senator Paul Simon, the sitting US Senator and a former Washington loyalist, on board. Paul Simon was described by Al Kindle as an 'Illinois' Ted Kennedy. Simon had taken the coalition that Harold Washington had constructed in Chicago and added small-town Illinois. His support was essential if Obama was going to be able to work around the Daley machine. Secondly, Obama had to lay low, quietly build his support, so that he had a solid base should Blair Hull try to use his political muscle to knock him out of the game. Finally, once he had gone public, he had to quickly and decisively energise the liberal and youth vote which was well represented in his state senatorial district, again another tactic out of the Harold Washington playbook.

Senator Paul Simon had been planning to endorse Barack Obama but he died during a heart operation. His backing still came when his daughter, Sheila Simon, agreed to go ahead with an endorsement in a 'cut from the same cloth' advert. In a later Axelrod campaign ad, Obama was compared to both Harold Washington and Paul Simon. Still, a flurry of polls in February to March 2004 showed Obama and Hynes level-pegging and Blair Hull between 5 percent and 14 percent ahead of them both.*

---

*John S. Jackson, *The Making of a Senator: Barack Obama and the 2004 Illinois Senate Race*, http://www.siu.edu/~ppi/PDF/papers/ Obama.pdf. pp. 7–8.

Then in March disaster struck for Hull who was already moving towards spending $29 million on the primary. When his divorce papers were published, they revealed that his former wife had obtained two restraining orders against him and that there had been a minor physical altercation.* Obama subsequently swept the board in Chicago and its surrounding suburban counties, winning the primary by 53 percent to Dan Hynes' 24 percent.

Amazingly, following the primary, Barack Obama had another stroke of luck relating to the divorce of his Republican opponent, Jack Ryan, another independently wealthy former financier. A court in California ruled that his divorce file should be opened and in the file were rather damaging revelations concerning his sex life. Given that the file was opened after the primary race, the Republicans embarrassingly had to switch their candidate and, bizarrely, drafted in the social conservative African-American Alan Keyes from Maryland. Whatever woolly strategic thinking went into that decision, it spectacularly backfired. Obama became US Senator by a margin of 70 percent to 27 percent.

During the campaign, Barack Obama became a national figure and that was just as important in propelling him forwards politically as his Senate victory. He had been asked by John Kerry to give the keynote address to the Democratic Convention in Boston. His speech electrified the crowd and seemed to capture the

---

*John S. Jackson. p. 9.

spirit of the times, an America beginning to weary of division, when he forthrightly said, 'There's not a liberal America and a conservative America – there's the *United States of America*. There's not a black America and white America and Latino America and Asian America; there's the United States of America.'* Straight away, people were talking about Barack Obama as a future President.

Having the possibility of attaining the highest office in the land before you is one thing, to actively set about it as soon as you enter Congress is quite another. That is exactly what his aides David Axelrod, Robert Gibbs and Pete Rouse did almost the minute he arrived in Washington. They put together a strategy for a run on presidency as early as 2008, which they called 'The Plan.'†

The Senator himself got down to the work of bedding himself down in Washington. He secured a position on the Foreign Relations Committee where, following the Democrats' Senate victory in 2006 he would serve under the Chairmanship of Senator Joe Biden from January 2007. He enjoyed early legislative success on anti-nuclear proliferation legislation in conjunction with Republican Indiana Senator Dick Lugar and also introduced legislation on transparency arrangements for Federal expenditure.

It was during his freshman year in the Senate that

---

*http://www.barackobama.com/2004/07/27/keynote_address_at_the_2004_de.php
†David Mendell, p. 305.

Obama's subtle voice on the sensitive issue of race was heard. When the levees failed after Hurricane Katrina hit New Orleans in August 2005, the whole world was horrified that such a loss of life could occur in the USA. Around two thousand people perished as much through malignant neglect as active malice. Whatever the root cause of this avoidable tragedy, the scale of fatality, the devastation of lives, the communal and national shock, emphasised one underlying reality. The African-American communities who were devastated in New Orleans were poor and segregated. They, like the residents of Altgeld Gardens, had borne the brunt of their own storm, in both cases economic; yet here was an actual, category three one.

Obama saw the tragedy as one of race and class. Class interplayed with race so that when tragedy struck, when the people of New Orleans were not able to get out for financial reasons and fear of dispossession as much as for reasons of practical planning, the weaknesses of America's society were exposed for the whole world to see.

These New Orleans people were not on the Bush administration's radar, their lives were not understood, and that had its roots in historical indifference. Barack Obama was walking a fine line between race and class, history and politics. He said of this process: 'I think there is a generational shift taking place in how values that are important to the African-American community are expressed in a way that builds bridges with other communities … I actually have felt very comfortable speaking on issues that are of particular importance to the African-American community, without losing focus on my primary task, which is to represent all the people of Illinois.'*

Obama had engaged in a search for his identity in his adolescence and early adult life, one that seemed to resolve itself some time around his experiences in South Chicago or soon after. Now he was articulating another search for identity. He was looking to express his understanding of the intersection of race and politics and how to make that meaningful to contemporary America in a way that was neither stuck in the past nor projecting too far forward. This search and articulation sat alongside his political development, never too far away, but not often on the surface. His old sparring partner in the Illinois Senate, Rickey Hendon, is working on a book titled, *Black Enough, White Enough: The Obama Dilemma*. To move beyond such a retrograde dualism is a challenge that Obama has set himself. He has navigated it with considerable dexterity.

❧

There is a fundamental dilemma in racial politics that every black politician looking to win anything other than local elections has to face. On the one hand, you have a need to move beyond a politics that is defined solely by racial history. Such racial exclusivity is a

---

*David Mendell, p. 320.

dishonest route for a politician. It fails to acknowledge where progress has taken place and it holds both the people you purport to represent and the wider community back. On the other hand, there are, in America, very tangible social and economic consequences of the history of segregation as well as the psychological humiliation of slavery. These can't simply be glossed over as they are real and must be addressed if you are to govern effectively.

Actually, the racial complex at the centre of American politics is of universal consequence. Some people are sucked into it, some react to it. The reality though is that as a black politician, though you may feel it grossly unjust, and it is, you still have to contend with these basic issues in a way that others do not. If you fail to find a clear message on these contentions then you are a sitting duck for a fear-based campaign against you. At the other end of the spectrum, you may well simply be dismissed as a sell-out. Without strong reserves of articulate reasoning, intellectual engagement and subtle communication, it becomes impossible to face the community or the nation with an argument that will endure.

The conservative writer, Shelby Steele, a mixed race, African-American like Barack Obama, thrust himself into the centre of the debate about these challenges facing black politicians early in the campaign with his overly-deterministically titled book, *A Bound Man: Why We Are Excited by Obama and Why He Can't Win*. Though his argument was dismissed by liberals as the ramblings of a sell-out and hoovered up by the right and more conservative Democrats as further evidence of an alleged vapidity on Obama's part, Steele's arguments struck to the core of the dilemma whilst proving to be completely wrong.

His basic point was that black candidates (and other upwardly mobile African-Americans) have two choices, to be 'challengers', those who reprimand white America for past crimes and accuse it of racism until proved otherwise, and to be 'bargainers', who forgive America's past crimes but then fail to be true to themselves and so simply become a receptacle for projected desire. The bargainer label appears in other forms such as 'post racial', more likely to be heard amongst those who applaud the political bargainer than those who are critical of it. Steele placed Jesse Jackson and Al Sharpton in the former category and Barack Obama amongst the bargainers. As he put it, 'You can't win by giving people a fuzzy feeling.'*

This argument had a fundamental flaw. It assumed that a candidate such as Barack Obama could not display an understanding of history, how it had played out, where things had changed and improved, and on that basis propose an argument that could address the concerns of the American people as whole. He was right in the sense that Barack Obama could not win as a 'challenger', as had been proved through the presidential campaigns of Jesse Jackson Sr and Al Sharpton, and was

---

*Shelby Steele, National Public Radio, December 4, 2007.

extremely unlikely to win as a shallow bargainer, and that even if he did win on such a platform would fail to govern effectively. Many people made a similar argument (including, most bizarrely, the chairman of the British Equality and Human Rights Commission who echoed Steele's argument*) pointing out that if Obama won it would actually be a *setback* for racial equality in the US: discrimination would be shielded with an African-American in the White House because Obama, as a bargainer, would not be able to address racial issues without losing the support of those who had entrusted him not to simply pursue a minority agenda.

If there were only bargainers and challengers then the argument may have some force but that is not the case. What if there was a third category of black politician? We could call them 'unifiers' but the label is less important than what they would represent and how they would conduct themselves in practice. They would acknowledge the past, look for its impact on the present, understand the fears and anxieties of those who are threatened by social change, but ultimately look for an agenda that could join the dots of common concern while addressing identifiable discrimination head on.

The reality that Obama acknowledges is that there has been considerable improvement in the economic success of African-Americans since the civil rights movement. Whereas just over 30 percent of black households were in the top 60 percent of income

---

*Trevor Phillips, *Prospect*, March 2008.

brackets in 1959, around 40 percent are now. Given the growth in the African-American population that represents a significant improvement for millions of families. Much of this improvement is testament to the impact of the civil rights movement (as a proportion of families in the upper 60 percent of incomes things have been relatively static since 1980). 41 percent of black families regard themselves as middle class compared with around 15 percent at the beginning of the 1960s.*

When compared to white incomes the picture is again mixed. Relative to white incomes there were big gains in black incomes until the late 1970s but the median full-time weekly earnings of black men stood at 78 percent of those of white men in 2004. Black and white men aged 30–39, for example, saw a decline in their median incomes from 1975 to 2005 with black men receiving $4,000 less and white men declining by almost $2,000.†

Three main factors hit black families hardest: the number of single parent families, low employment rates in black communities and an educational divide caused by bad schooling and the costs of higher education. This is the legacy of segregation. Poorer families are more

---

*Douglas J. Besharov, *The Economic Stagnation of the Black Middle Class (Relative to Whites)*, American Enterprise Institute/ University of Maryland. Presentation before US Commission on Civil Rights, July 15, 2005.
†Julia B. Isaacs, Isabel V. Sawhill, and Ron Haskins, *Getting Ahead or Losing Ground: Economic Mobility in America*, The Brookings Institution.

likely to be single parent (it's a chicken and egg question as to which came first, the poverty or the family breakdown?), they are more likely to live in ghettoised or concentrated communities facing economic decline (as was seen in Altgeld Gardens), and they have poorer education provision as a result of the way of financing education in the USA as well as the impact of wider social issues.

On this basis, it is hasty to rush, in challenger style, to the conclusion that income disparities are *ipso facto* the consequences of ongoing racial discrimination, though it is not a factor we can eliminate. These disparities are, however, certainly the *legacy* of racial discrimination mixed with America's tendency to embed social exclusion as a result of insufficient corrective measures.

Obama himself confronted the complexities of race in modern America in *The Audacity of Hope*. He acknowledged the persistent gap between the median incomes of black and white families though he also noted the considerable improvement since the 1960s with the large expansion of a black middle class. There was 'unfinished business' from the civil rights era. Discriminatory practice could still be seen in employment, housing and education and this needed to be confronted.

However, Obama was not willing to see it solely as a government problem. There was a need for individual responsibility also. He wrote, 'Many of the social or cultural factors that negatively affect black people, for example, simply mirror in exaggerated form problems

that afflict America as a whole: too much television …
too much consumption of poisons and a lack of empha-
sis on educational attainment.'

There were problems that were more prevalent in
black communities as a result of more extreme and
damaging cultural attitudes: 'Then there's the collapse
of the two-parent black household, a phenomenon that
is occurring at such an alarming rate when compared to
the rest of American society that what was once a difference in degree has become a difference in kind.'*

Ultimately, though, Barack Obama saw that the
problems afflicting black communities were similar to
those afflicting poor white communities such that the
issues might not be racial but rather economic. These
issues were downsizing, outsourcing, automation, wage
stagnation, the dismantling of employer-based health-
care and pension plans, and 'schools that fail to teach
young people the skills they need to compete in a global
economy.'

In all this, Barack Obama is neither in denial about
the legacy of America's racist past nor is he allowing
himself to be defined by it. His attitude is not 'post-
racial' nor is it racially resentful. He is refusing either to
turn the guilt of white America against it or to use those
feelings to propel himself forward. He is not harvesting
feelings of African-American victimhood in order to
swell his base. He is doing something very different. He
is engaging in a practical and historically aware analysis

---

*Barack Obama, *The Audacity of Hope*, pp. 244–245.

of the nation's problems in order to propose pragmatic solutions to meet a broad range of needs, both particular and general. This approach is neither challenger nor bargainer nor a clumsy and unsustainable combination of the two. Luckily, Shelby Steele is not the only racial theorist available. There is also Cornel West.

❦

Back in 1993, Cornel West wrote, in his succinct, honest and powerful book on the state of America's race relations and politics, *Race Matters*, 'The fundamental crisis in black America is twofold: too much poverty and too little self-love.'* For West, the world of black leadership was not divided into sell-outs and intransigents; it was just that the 1993 class of black leaders weren't up to the task of cracking the code of America's racial and economic inequality.

Cornel West is not just a random theorist. Barack Obama himself proclaimed him 'a genius, a public intellectual, a preacher, the oracle' in a fundraiser in Harlem on November 29, 2007.† In return Cornel West, at the same event, was gushing about Barack Obama's qualities and capabilities to be President. Beyond a mutual love in, Cornel West's ideas can be read in concurrence which many of Barack Obama's own perspectives on contemporary race relations in the USA.

---

*Cornel West, *Race Matters*, p. 93.
†*http://uk.youtube.com/watch?v=U7H5irpvrjY&NR=1*

There are two essential elements to understanding Cornel West's analysis. Firstly, the ideology and practice of white supremacy have left such an indelible mark on every area of American life that the litmus test for American democracy is the elimination of those divides. He echoes and contemporises W.E.B. Du Bois in asserting that, 'The problem of the twenty-first century remains the problem of the colour line.' But then he goes on to write, and this is the second foundational point of importance, 'Racial progress is undeniable in America … Glass ceilings have been pierced – not smashed – by extraordinary persons of colour. Overt forms of discrimination have been attacked and forced to become more covert.'*

For West, neither conservatives nor liberals possess all the answers and this is the message that Barack Obama has taken to heart. Liberals focus naïvely on the economic angle alone. More government expenditure or more government programmes will not do the trick in this incomplete and ineffective creed. Conservatives, in their behaviourism, highlight some of the shortcomings of individuals that hold them, their families and their communities back. Where conservatives fail is in understanding the structural causes that condition the lack of personal responsibility.

There is little point in challenging an individual's behaviour unless you are willing to give them the opportunity to lift themselves and their family up.

---

*Cornel West, p. xiv (2001 edition).

Structure and behaviour are inseparable as are institutions and values. Fail to understand that and we will continue to lock the dispossessed into deprivation. The social emancipation of African-Americans occurred just as the economy was sundering the low-skilled, working class away from the rest due to technological and economic change. This is the dual crisis – racial and economic – and a burgeoning middle class and a desperate underclass is the consequence of this stratification. A kind of nihilism is left amongst those who are dispossessed, a collective despair individually felt.

To confront this nihilism, there is the need for leadership initiating a 'politics of conversion.' This needs to happen at the local level. At one point, West even writes, 'This new leadership must be grounded in grassroots organising ... Whoever our leaders will be as we approach the twenty-first century, their challenge will be to help Americans determine whether a genuine multiracial democracy can be created and sustained in an era of global economy and a moment of xenophobic frenzy.'*

Who will these leaders be? Cornel West, from the window of 1993, saw three types of black leader. There were the 'race-effacing managerial leaders' ('bargainers' in Steele's vernacular) such as Tom Bradley, former Mayor of Los Angeles, who survive on 'political savvy and personal diplomacy.' By 'casting the mainstream as the only game in town' they stunt progressive

*Cornel West, p. 13.

development. Secondly, there are the 'race-identifying protest leaders' (again, there are parallels here with Steele's 'challengers'). Then there is a third category, the race-transcending prophetic leaders.

Such figures are rare. As West describes it, 'To be an elected official and prophetic leader requires personal integrity and political savvy, moral vision and prudential judgement, courageous defiance and organisational patience.'* Although it cannot be said with certainty whether Cornel West regards Barack Obama as such a politician, he did describe him at the Harlem fundraiser as 'An eloquent brother, a good brother, and he aspires to leadership just as the American empire is in crisis … character and judgement trumps all the pseudo-rhetoric about experience. We love him for his vocation, his poise and his vision.' He went on to explain that, to use a musical analogy, people shouldn't dismiss Obama just as they wouldn't dismiss John Coltrane because he isn't Johnny Hodges or Alicia Keys because she isn't Ella Fitzgerald. One figure that Cornel West did place in the 'race-transcending prophetic leader' category was Harold Washington. At the very least, it seems likely that Cornel West sees the potential in Barack Obama to achieve this status.

West demands nothing short of a 'democratic awakening.' His call is for the type of leadership that America has enjoyed periodically in its history: in the 1860s in the face of civil war and abolition of slavery, in the 1890s as it confronted imperial greed, in the 1930s as it dealt

---

*Cornel West, p. 61.

with economic depression and in the 1960s as it finally faced its racial and economic injustice. America needs such leadership now, as West wrote, to 'take their country back from the hands of corrupted plutocratic and imperial elites.'*

As America contends with issues of race in the twenty-first century, Cornel West is a liberating public intellectual. His contribution, and there is little doubt that he has had a degree of influence on Barack Obama's thinking, is in facilitating a movement away from the old daggers drawn, divided way of looking at these issues. What he doesn't seek is to deny or bury the real issues of racial division that remain. Inevitably, Barack Obama has had to publicly contend with this dilemma also. With the perpetual background hum of race during the primary campaign, he took the decision to finally confront it head-on. He did so in the birthplace of the American republic, Philadelphia, and gave the best speech of the campaign.

❧

Comparisons between Abraham Lincoln and Barack Obama have almost become clichéd. Both were single term members of Congress (Lincoln in the House of Representatives and Obama in the Senate), both were lawyers from Illinois, and occasionally articulated their arguments in aloof lawyerly fashion. They represented

---

*Cornel West, *Democracy Matters*, p. 23.

a challenge to the existing order and were accused of inexperience as a consequence, though they both defeated more experienced rivals in their party's primaries. In Lincoln's case his election would precipitate the break up of the Union and the Civil War. Obama's election is not be nearly so dramatic but it does mark a point of departure in American history. As a modern Democrat his electoral support has at its core a similar territorial grab as the Republican Lincoln's did in 1860: the Republican won on the basis of victory in the Midwest, Northeast and Pacific West.

Both faced accusations during their primary campaigns based on their associations, in Obama's case with his pastor, the fiery and uncompromising Reverend Jeremiah Wright, and in Lincoln's case an alleged link with a radical, direct action emancipationist, John Brown. The historian Gary Wills has compared the response of both men in the form of two speeches with an appeal to the constitution as their defining feature. Lincoln's was delivered to Cooper Union in New York on February 27, 1860 and Obama's was delivered in the National Constitution Center in Philadelphia, on March 18, 2008.*

Both men faced very different racial controversies. Abraham Lincoln had to deflect all manner of extreme accusations about his designs and associations from Southern slave-owners and Northern Democrats, most notably the man who had defeated him in a famous Senatorial race in 1858, Senator Stephen Douglas. In

---

*Gary Wills, *New York Review of Books*, May 1, 2008.

Obama's case, his embarrassment wasn't so much to do with the positions that he was adopting, it was more to do with the radical statements disdainful of America made by the pastor of his church. One dealt with an existential threat. The other contended with a political threat. Both speeches had a central role in keeping each man on the road to his party's nomination.

Lincoln's argument was, in essence, very simple. When the likes of Senator Douglas claimed constitutional authority, they should ensure that it was based on the facts. The notion that the framers of the constitution either explicitly protected the right to own slaves or protected the rights of states from Federal authority to prohibit slave ownership was demonstrably false. He showed it quite plainly. He analysed in detail the voting records of the thirty-nine men who had signed the constitution and found that the majority had voted in some measure to restrict the rights of states on the slavery issue. If their purpose was to respect the rights of states in this regard then they would not have voted in this way. Abolition, if democratically determined, was, therefore, constitutional.

He rejected the notion of any association with John Brown. It was either a fact or it was not fact. Let the accusers produce the evidence if it were factual, if they could not then they were making unfounded and scurrilous accusations. Lincoln brushed off the threat that should a Republican President be elected then that would force the South to secede. Using a wicked turn of humour he mocked them thus, 'A highwayman holds a pistol to my ear, and mutters through his teeth, "Stand and deliver, or I shall kill you, and then you will be a murderer!"'*

The speech received rave reviews in New York, the backyard of one of his close competitors in the Republican race, William Seward, and Lincoln went on to win the nomination.

Rather than delving into to the motivations of the founding fathers, Barack Obama went to their originating text, the US Constitution. A document that was 'signed but ultimately unfinished,' it contained the promise of equality, liberty, justice and a union that was to be perfected over time. That notion of perfectibility had led, in Obama's words, to the 'Long march of those who came before us, a march for a more just, more equal, more free, more caring and more prosperous America.'†
That said, he refused to be perceived through a purely racial lens as some had tried to marginalise him.

He rejected the outdated views of Reverend Jeremiah Wright. America had 'never really worked through' the complexities of race but the results of Jim Crow segregation were everywhere to see: poor educational attainment in schools that had been segregated, legal discrimination that prevented many black families from building the assets they needed to climb ladders out of poverty, a lack of economic opportunity, and the poorer

---

* *http://showcase.netins.net/web/creative/lincoln/speeches/cooper.htm*
† *http://www.barackobama.com/2008/03/18/remarks_of_senator_barack_obam_53.php*

services that urban, black communities received. All of this helped to create a 'cycle of violence, blight and neglect that continues to haunt us.' Equally, the anger and frustrations of white communities that were finding life tough needed to be understood.

In Obama's view the mistake that Wright made was a failure to understand the progress that had been established. America had not only changed but it had demonstrated that it could change. Nonetheless, the legacy of discrimination and, 'current incidents of discrimination – while less overt than in the past – are real and must be addressed.'

Schools need investment, civil rights need to be enforced, there needs to be greater fairness in the criminal justice system and new 'ladders of opportunity' need to be erected. He sent out a clarion call for the election to be about the issues, the common challenges that America faced, rather than the issues that divided it.

Reverend Wright did not go quietly, responding to Obama's speech with a tour of TV studios and a round of speeches. Obama was more effective in defining America's racial challenges than dealing with his Reverend Wright issue but was more powerful for that. In the end, Barack Obama had to push his pastor, in the media vernacular, 'under a bus' and sever all his links with him by rejecting, denouncing, abhorring his continued attacks on America.

Barack Obama's dilemmas over how to handle the explosive issue of race expose fissures that still exist in

American politics despite the argument that somehow he was given an easy ride by the press as a consequence of his colour. This argument doesn't really stand up to scrutiny. The bar is higher for black candidates seeking election in a multi-racial environment. It is not so high that it can't be vaulted, as many have proved, but it is easy to understand the frustration that there is an extra trust test that they have to face which white candidates, all other things being equal, do not.

America has concentrated pockets of racism just as it has concentrated pockets of urban poverty. In political terms, this can have an impact. Barack Obama's difficulties in the Appalachian states during the primaries have been ascribed to just such a concentration of, if not overt racism, then a lack of racial trust. He struggled in Pennsylvania – though that turned decisively his way during the election itself – as well as in Ohio, West Virginia and Kentucky.*

During the primary campaign, there was a constant reference to the 'Tom Bradley effect' as an argument against Barack Obama's nomination. This referred to the alleged over counting of support for the African-American Mayor of Los Angeles in his Californian gubernatorial race with George Deukmejian in 1982. Victory was declared for Bradley on the night when exit polls pointed to a large victory. He inexplicably lost and the theory, which has proved to be utter nonsense, was

---

*http://www.dhinmi.dailykos.com/storyonly/2008/5/12/134251/930/338/514258

that white voters were telling the pollsters one thing and doing another in the privacy of the booth.

That is not what happened at all. The polls showed a narrow race right up until polling day as Tom Bradley's pollster has since explained.* What happened was that exit polls in 1982 were methodologically inaccurate, in, for example, failing to count absentee ballots where Deukmejian had resounding strength.

Despite the unsavoury hint behind the 'Bradley effect' argument, it proved to have no validity in the 2008 race either. A study into the 2008 primary race found that Senator Obama was performing by an average of 1.4 percent *better* than his poll ratings suggested.† Not only was there no 'Bradley effect' but, it would seem, one could speculate through superior organisation, Obama was over-performing.

This 'Bradley effect' argument was just one of the means used to discredit Senator Obama's campaign. Other means included the Reverend Jeremiah Wright's suggestive accusations, the constant references to him not being up to the formidable Republican attack machine, the articulation that he couldn't appeal to Hispanic voters or working-class white communities, and the attempts to marginalise him as a candidate

---

*http://www.realclearpolitics.com/articles/2008/10/the_bradley_effect_selective_m.html

†Daniel J Hopkins, *No More Wilder Effect, Never a Whitman Effect: When and Why Polls Mislead about Black and Female Candidates*, Department of Government, Harvard University.

with sectional appeal, particularly just after his stunning victory in South Carolina when President Clinton dismissed his campaign as a 'fairytale'.

Despite the attempts to insinuate negativity and define him through his race, he was able to come through all of it. The simple fact is that, as the Philadelphia speech demonstrated, Barack Obama is a candidate who is rooted in racial identity but not exclusively defined by it. He is neither post-racial nor a bargainer. He is himself and he will define himself in his own terms.

Obama stands at the head of a cadre of young, ambitious and highly talented black politicians such as Deval Patrick, Cory Booker and Adrian Fenty. They have faced these dilemmas their whole political careers and will continue to face them. There is an injustice in that but, should they handle it well, they may just be the stronger for it. Time will tell whether they too can navigate a path through the false dichotomy of challenger versus bargainer status. Obama's subtle articulation of these issues is a marker. They will also want to move quickly beyond racial political stereotyping as Barack Obama did. For that, they need a campaign like Obama '08. It was certainly the strongest Democratic campaign in decades. It has also spawned a movement for change.

6

Becoming President

DESPITE ITS UNEXPECTEDNESS, there was a poetic simplicity to Barack Obama winning the Democratic nomination. He set his strategy, kept to it, understood the rules of the nomination from state to state, and focused on building an organisation that began to take on movement characteristics. Controlled by a small group of advisers, people like David Axelrod, David Plouffe, Robert Gibbs and Stephen Hildebrand, the strategy was clear and ruthless and the execution precise. They understood the game and they played it hard from start to finish. Obama was the opportunity and the campaign translated that opportunity into reality.

In early 2007, the notion that Barack Obama would walk away with his party's nomination seemed fanciful, though not entirely ridiculous. If Hillary Clinton had a campaign that matched her appeal as a potential nominee, then it was probable that she would have won.

Even with a campaign that was ramshackle, internally

divided, poorly managed and flailing, at least until early March 2008 (which was too late to turn the situation around for her), she received 18 million votes, and had 48 percent of the pledged delegates to her name. It is part of Barack Obama's fortune as a politician that he has faced a series of opponents who have either self-destructed, as happened twice in his Senate campaign, or have been unequal to the organisational challenge.

Hillary Clinton's campaign, unworthy of her qualities as a candidate, was off the pace right from the start. They were expecting the turnout in the Iowan caucus to be in the region of 150,000 but the mobilising success of the Obama campaign ensured that 230,000 voters caucused.* That was critical in establishing him as Hillary Clinton's main rival for the nomination. He won and suddenly his candidacy was electrifying the Democratic race. Just five days later, however, Hillary Clinton had a comeback victory in New Hampshire (following the famous 'weepy' moment in a television interview). Her campaign was quick to claim the victory as a game-changer.†

Hillary Clinton's after this brief new dawn then experiencing a number of blows in quick succession. By moving their primaries forward, Michigan and Florida had their delegates removed from the nomination vote by the Democratic National Committee (DNC). They were two significant states accounting for 311 pledged

---

*Jay Newton-Small, *Time Magazine*, September 10, 2008.
†Joshua Green, *Atlantic Magazine*, September 2008.

delegates between them in a contest that required 2110 votes for victory. It should be noted that Obama was not on the ballot in the Michigan primary. Nonetheless, the eventual decision of the DNC Rules and Bylaws Committee to return half votes to all the delegates of these two states could not compensate Clinton for the momentum that could have come from victory in them.

By the time Super Tuesday came along on February 5th, when twenty-two states and American Samoa would be voting, Obama had scored a good victory in South Carolina nudging him into a pledged delegate lead overall. The major tactical error of the Clinton campaign was about to become clear. They had put all their eggs into the Super Tuesday basket, expecting that the 'inevitability' of their candidate would be underlined on that February day. With the campaign $6 million in the red they had also run out of cash. Obama's message of 'change' was trumping Clinton's 'experience' and the Clinton campaign had little to fight back with as of early February.

Though Clinton secured eye-catching victories in California and New York, Super Tuesday left Barack Obama with an overall pledged delegate lead of thirteen. Obama was holding his own in terms of momentum, and, even worse, Clinton's campaign had no real plan for the post-Super Tuesday campaign. It was at this point that Barack Obama pulled into a commanding and pretty insurmountable lead.

Powering ahead in February, he won eleven consecutive caucuses and primaries. His large 180 to 60 pledged delegate victory in the Chesapeake primaries (Maryland, Virginia and Washington, DC) was particularly impressive. It became clear that if he won in either Ohio or Texas the race was pretty much at its conclusion.

At around this time there was growing concern amongst Democrats about a prolonged race and the impact of a divisive battle between two candidates who were both strong but neither strong enough to land the knockout blow. These concerns became more acute when the Clinton campaign went strongly negative in the run up to the Texas and Ohio primaries with a version of the '3 a.m. ad' – *Who do you want answering the phone in a national emergency?* – that Walter Mondale had run against his opponent for the 1984 nomination, the Colorado Senator Gary Hart.

When the race failed to close on March 4th after Hillary Clinton won both Texas and Ohio, the already loud concerns about the harm that such a race might do to the Democrats' chances became a cacophony. The remainder of the race became a trading of blows between the two campaigns. Clinton actually managed to secure 44 more pledged delegates than Obama in the final ten races but it was nowhere near enough.

The race hit some pretty low moments, with Obama, in particular, facing a tough ride when the Reverend Jeremiah Wright story hit a peak in March, and again in late April when Wright gave a speech to the National Press Club. Hillary herself occasionally over-stepped the mark, even at one point suggesting that while she and John McCain had been 'vetted', Barack Obama had not.

Despite this intense cross-fire between the Obama and Clinton camps there is little evidence that the tough and close battle did any harm to Barack Obama's candidacy. Indeed, the tricky issues that he had to face, such as references to his relationship with Antoin 'Tony' Rezko (who was found guilty of fraud and corruption during the campaign), Bill Ayers (who was involved with the terrorist organisation, the Weathermen Underground in the 1960s), and, of course, Jeremiah Wright himself, were comprehensively aired taking away much of their sting come November.

Some of Hillary Clinton's more robust questioning of Barack Obama's experience created a degree of difficulty down the line but not much. Bill Clinton's rousing endorsement at the Democratic Convention in August and on a number of occasions thereafter left the McCain campaign unable to use the Clintons against Barack Obama beyond the very early stages of the campaign. Most importantly, and this was to Barack Obama's advantage, the long campaign gave him ongoing momentum. John McCain had wrapped up the Republican nomination by March 4th. From that point onwards, he was nigh on invisible until August, whereas Barack Obama was still enjoying wall to wall coverage. At the end of the primary race, Barack Obama was two to three points ahead of McCain on average.*

More crucial than his poll lead, the presence of his campaign at full tilt in state after state had ensured that

---

*See *http://www.pollster.com/polls/us/08-us-pres-ge-mvo.php*

he was recruiting volunteers, building his donor list, raising his profile, and registering voters for the Democrats. The late primaries would include states such as Pennsylvania, Indiana and North Carolina, which would all become battleground states in the election proper. In a dozen key states – Ohio, Florida, Georgia, North Carolina, Virginia, Indiana, Missouri, Colorado, Iowa, Nevada, New Mexico and Pennsylvania – voter rolls were expanded by 4 million votes, the majority of these new voters being Democrats.

Primary turnout records were set by the Democrats in twenty-six out of fifty states. 36,731,478 voted in Democratic primaries with the Republican turnout hitting 20,613,383 as a result of the early finish of their process (Republicans have a winner-takes-all voting system whereas the Democrats have a more proportional system which can prolong their race).*

In Colorado and Nevada, new Democrats were registered by a margin of four to one over new Republicans, and in North Carolina, one of the late primaries, by a margin of six to one. In Nevada, a state won by a margin of 21,000 votes by George W. Bush in 2004, 91,000 Democrats were registered while the Republicans only added 22,000.† The race may have been fraught, occasionally bubbling over, but it had the

*The Primary Turnout Story, *American University* October 1, 2008. *http://www.american.edu/ia/cdem/csae/pdfs/csae081001.pdf*
† Alec MacGillis and Alice Crites, *Washington Post*, October 6, 2008.

nation gripped, helped get some of the dirty laundry out of the way before the election proper and mobilised the Obama campaign, giving it a head start over the McCain campaign.

As for the Clinton campaign, it increasingly faced a narrowing viable path to the nomination. Mark Penn, her chief strategist, outlined a forward strategy in a memo titled 'Path to Victory' on March 30th. Senator Clinton had to win Pennsylvania, West Virginia, Kentucky and Puerto Rico. She had to perform well in North Carolina, South Dakota, Montana and Guam. On top of that, she had to get Michigan and Florida seated at the Democratic Convention or secure a revote, be ahead in the popular vote (including Florida and Michigan), be ahead in delegates from primaries (as opposed to caucuses), lead Obama in head-to-head polls with John McCain, raise concern about Barack Obama's lack of coattails for congressional races, and convince super-delegates that Barack Obama was a 'doomsday scenario.' He then recommended a decisive shift to negative campaigning, including on the Jeremiah Wright issue, and that was the strategy that was adopted.*

The March 30th memo demonstrated the dire straits that the Hillary Clinton campaign was in. Much like John McCain would find himself in a position where he had to win every battleground state come November to have any chance of victory, the walls were clearly closing in on the Clinton campaign. To pull off the whole

---

*Joshua Green, *Atlantic Magazine*, September 2008.

list of Mark Penn's objectives was not impossible. It was just exceedingly unlikely and in the end the campaign ended up achieving about two of the ten objectives outlined.

Momentum was building up behind Barack Obama in a year that held the greatest prospect for a first-time, Democratic presidential candidate since Bill Clinton's election in 1992. In John McCain, a man with a powerful biography centring on his endurance in the face of torture in a Vietnamese Prisoner of War camp, the Republicans had chosen the candidate with the best chance of giving them victory. But there was still a better than evens chance of returning a Democratic candidate to the White House in 2008, even with John McCain as the Republican opponent.

⁂

The mid-term elections in 2006 were a stunning success for the Democrats. They won 31 House of Representative seats in the process taking control of it, and 5 seats to tie numbers in the Senate. Democrats also won the majority of gubernatorial elections. It was not a ringing endorsement for a radical and clear agenda. In 1994, when the Republicans swept home, there had been a clear route map, the Contract with America, the most radical right-wing agenda ever supported nationally.

Rather, the 2006 mid-terms were actually a large protest vote. According to the pollster Stanley Greenberg three-quarters of the 41 percent of voters who said that

Iraq was their most pressing concern voted Democrat.*

As the bloodshed gradually mounted in Iraq, and this on top of the disaster of Hurricane Katrina just a year previously, it seemed that the Bush administration was out of control and woefully short of competence. By the midterms Bush's approval rating was hovering around the -25 percent mark. While the majority of Americans considered Iraq to be the biggest problem facing the new Congress, 57 percent believed that the Democrats had no plan for resolving the issue.† The electoral success of 2006 was an anti-Bush rather than a pro-Democrat vote.

President Bush's approval ratings still continued to slide hitting a net approval of under -40 percent by the time of the 2008 election.‡ While Congress had an even worse approval rating as a body, sinking as low as -60 percent, the Democrats had an average lead of 8 percent heading into the election in 2008.§

Perhaps the most salient feature of the state of the nation's opinion throughout 2008 was the continually high numbers of voters who considered the nation to be on the 'wrong track.' By the 2008 election, the number of people who saw the country heading on the 'wrong track' was in the high 80s and occasionally hit the 90

---

*Matt Bai, *The Argument: Billionaires, Bloggers and the Battle to Remake Democratic Politics*, p. 286.

†Matt Bai, p. 287.

‡*http://www.pollster.com/polls/us/jobapproval-bush.php*

§*http://www.realclearpolitics.com/polls/#rcp-avg-904*

percent mark. This election was about change and who could make the most convincing case that they and their platform embodied change. Would it be the 'maverick' Senate veteran from Arizona who had made a habit of getting up the noses of his own party or would it be the freshman Senator from Illinois with the cool temperament and a charismatic political groove?

The Obama campaign so determinedly tried to tie McCain to the George W. Bush presidency because if he could be characterised as 'Bush Mark III' then it would be almost impossible for him to win. It was a good year not to be the incumbent. Underneath the contemporary state of political affairs there also lay longer-term factors that the Democrats, with the right candidates and a strong campaign, would benefit from. These factors were economic and demographic and the two factors were interplaying with one another.

In an echo of Kevin Phillips' prophetic *The Emerging Republican Majority*, published in 1969 in the aftermath of Richard Nixon's first electoral victory, John B. Judis and Ruy Teixeira published *The Emerging Democratic Majority* in 2002. With Al Gore's defeat in 2000 still fresh in people's minds, it was a brave argument to make that a new era of Democratic dominance was imminent. The argument seemed to lose further credibility when the Democrats lost again in 2004.

Though Judis and Texeira's assumed the Democrats would win elections, this is not what their argument was about. Election victories ultimately depend on contingent factors as much as underlying ones but environments that are more favourable to one party over another can be observed independently of what happens in any given election. When the Democrats unexpectedly won in 1992 they'd done so by selecting the best political communicator of his generation, the economy was tanking, George H. W. Bush appeared aloof in the face of economic strife, and the decision of Ross Perot to run as an independent ate into the Republican vote in state after state. Clinton's triangulation strategy positioned him well in strategic terms and that was necessary for victory. George W. Bush won in 2004 both as a consequence of the ongoing 'War on Terror' and a devastatingly effective campaign waged by Karl Rove.

America is changing. As Judis and Texeira put it, 'Beginning in the 1920s, the United States began to shift toward a post-industrial economy in which the production of ideas and services would dominate the production of goods.'* Such an economy is characterised by a high number of people engaged in high-skill, professional, service-based industries.

They live in 'ideopolises', new cities that revolve around the 'production of ideas', where the suburbs and central metropolitan areas blend into one in a seamless web of work and home, where there are universities, health services, manufacturing, financial services, health clubs, coffee bars, book shops and retail parks.

---

*John B. Judis and Ruy Texeira, *The Emerging Democratic Majority*, p. 8.

The 'ideopolis' value set, shared by white, working-class voters as well as more affluent voters, is socially liberal, believes in public investment, services, regulation and is socially concerned. These ideopolises are growing: Denver-Boulder, Multnomah County, Oregon, Mercer County in which Princeton University is located and Seattle's King County, are typical examples. 'Ideopolis' voters comprised 43.7 percent nationally in 2000 and the Democrats secured 55 percent of their vote even in the election of that year.*

Ethnic demographics are shifting too. The America of Richard Nixon was 84 percent non-Hispanic white. It is now only 68 percent non-Hispanic white. This has real electoral consequences. George W. Bush's 'compassionate conservatism' was designed mainly as a defensive move to split middle-ground voters. Latinos though were targeted vigorously. By 2004, George W. Bush secured 40 percent of the Latino vote and that was critical in states such as Texas, New Mexico, Nevada and Florida.† In 2008, the Latino vote was 10 percent of the total.

There is perhaps no better example of this social, economic and demographic change than Colorado. The state is 8 percent Latino. The Denver-Boulder area of Denver is a prime example of an ideopolis and Al

---

*John B. Judis and Ruy Texeira, pp. 76–77.
†Hispanics Rising II, *An Overview of the Growing Power of America's Hispanic Community*, New Democratic Network. http:// www.ndn.org/hispanic/hispanicsrising-ii.pdf

Gore carried it in 2000 despite not even campaigning there.* Colorado itself has only been won once since 1964 by the Democrats and that was in 1992 when Ross Perot's strong standing there, as a result of his campaign's resources and his appeal to 'a plague on both your houses' Independents and moderate Republicans, prevented George H. W. Bush from winning the state. His son won the state by over 4.5 percent in 2004. In 2008, it was mightily competitive.

Colorado's population is 19 percent Catholic and 23 percent evangelical yet the Democratic Governor Bill Ritter won the state in 2006 not through an appeal based on religiously constructed social values. Instead, he was able to win the state by seventeen points by proposing a moderate agenda and, without posing as a religious right candidate (despite being a Roman Catholic himself), reassuring religious voters that he took their concerns seriously. He has not sought to overturn abortion laws in the state and instead his agenda focuses on environmental issues, the green economy, universal healthcare and welfare measures. He is the embodiment of the 'progressive centralism' that Judis and Texeira suggest will have the right appeal in the new America. And in 2008, Barack Obama won Colorado by a street, 53 percent to 45 percent.

For those who don't live in these new ideopolises, the economic changes in the last few decades have had a negative or non-positive impact. The consequences of

---

*John B. Judis and Ruy Texeira, p. 74.

economic change on static communities, as has been seen in Chicago, can be catastrophic. Robert Reich, former Secretary of Labor under President Bill Clinton, describes the new economic paradigm as 'supercapitalism.' But it certainly is not super if you have been left behind and that is what has happened in many of America's old industrial towns.

Supercapitalism has come about as the result of the increasing deregulation of the economy, driven by an increasing corporate influence on politics, and rapid technological change over the last few decades. In practice, this has (up until the credit crunch) been good for investors, consumers and senior executives who benefit from competition, but less good for workers. The benefits of increasing productivity have not been passed on, going to senior executives and shareholders rather than the average worker.

From 1974 to 2004 the lowest fifth of the population saw only a 2.8 percent real increase in their salaries compared to the 63.6 percent that the top fifth have seen. The average CEO now earns over 350 times the average worker's take home pay where the ratio thirty years ago was nearer to forty times.*

The failure of workers to be rewarded proportionately for their increased productivity is one thing but their non-pay benefits and job security have also suffered. Income volatility is now double what it was thirty years ago, personal bankruptcy is up by a factor of six since

---

*Robert B. Reich, *Supercapitalism*, pp. 103–109.

1980, and the mortgage foreclosure rate had gone up by 500 percent between the early 1970s and 2005 (before the sub-prime mortgage crisis!). As corporations have cut back on benefits an increasing number of Americans spend periods of time without health insurance, and the scaling back of pension benefits has resulted in larger numbers investing in more risky defined-contribution rather than defined-benefit pensions.*

This rise in insecurity is part of what Jacob Hacker has described as 'the great risk shift' from corporations to individuals and it has left Middle America fearing for its economic future.

There was little doubt that Middle America was hurting during 2008. Stanley Greenberg went back to Macomb County, the quintessential Reagan Democrat territory, to see how things had changed from 1985 when he did his initial survey there. He found that these voters, though they did still have strong views on race, were not allowing that to determine how they voted in the 2008 election.

It was obvious to Greenberg on this re-tread that the economy was the real impassioned concern of these mainly white, blue-collar, Catholic voters. Surrogate issues for race such as welfare, crime, reverse discrimination and Detroit were never mentioned in the discussion about why the country and state were off track. The problem was the economy and they blamed George W. Bush, the North American Free Trade Agreement,

*Jacob S. Hacker, *The Great Risk Shift*, p. 2 and pp. 12–14.

Jennifer Granholm (Governor of Michigan) and the automakers.*

Convincing these voters of his ability to manage the economy and building trust in his leadership qualities were essential to Barack Obama's success with the very voters that the Democrats have had such difficulty attracting since the Nixon era. Events were to give him an opportunity to show his qualities as the global financial system collapsed into chaos from the second week of September when the US Government refused to prevent the bankruptcy of the investment bank, Lehman Brothers.

Just a couple of weeks prior to the onset of the so-called 'credit crunch', John McCain had selected the Governor of Alaska, Sarah Palin, as his running mate. Her appeal was calculated to be to the Republican base, independent voters and former Hillary Clinton voters such as the blue-collar workers in Macomb County. In the event, the tactic, like so much else in the McCain campaign, was exceptionally flawed. Barack Obama won Macomb County by 36,109 votes according to exit polls. John Kerry had lost it by 6,006 votes in 2004.

Palin did succeed in shoring up the Republican base but her supposed appeal to Independents beyond the base was limited. Obama's lead amongst Independents and amongst women, the latter condescended by the notion that they would vote for a woman on the basis that

---

*Stanley B. Greenberg, James Carville, Andrew Baumann, Karl Agne and Jesse Contario, *Back to Macomb: Reagan Democrats and Barack Obama*, p. 16.

she was a woman, continued to rise and Sarah Palin soon became a net drag on the McCain ticket. Her woeful performances in one-on-one interviews where her desperate lack of knowledge of core issues was exposed failed to convince voters that she was ready to be Vice President.

Despite an above par performance in the vice presidential debate against the experienced Senator Joe Biden and some good performances on the stump, Sarah Palin was palpably not ready or maybe even capable of serving in the second highest office of the land. When economic crisis hit, the lack of substance on the McCain-Palin ticket would add, in unseen ways, to John McCain's difficulties.

John McCain made matters worse for himself by vacillating over his response to the crisis. First the fundamentals of the economy were 'sound' then the US was in crisis all in the course of a single day. He then suspended his campaign to return to Washington in order to broker a deal on a rescue package now that a series of major banks and insurers were in jeopardy and the world's largest insurer, AIG, had been taken over by the Federal Government. But it turned out that John McCain was becoming an obstacle to a deal rather than a broker. His campaign never did really suspend its activities.

A turning point in the campaign had been reached and Barack Obama's cool temperament hit the right note in the midst of a fraught economic episode. His poll lead started to widen and his debate performances, focused directly on America's middle-classes, were reassuring exactly those voters who had some initial doubts about his ability to lead. In contrast, McCain was running a pretty standard Republican attack campaign. Only this time it didn't work; the old tricks were water off the national economic crisis duck's back.

The long-term factors were in place – a woefully unpopular President, economic and demographic change that was favouring the Democrats – and now the short-term factors were breaking in Barack Obama's favour also. The candidate was performing exceptionally well under the pressure. The final element of a Democratic victory was the quality of the campaign. As it happened, the Barack Obama campaign, which had assumed a number of movement type characteristics, was perhaps equal to anything devised by Lee Atwater or Karl Rove. It was a movement for change and its force was relentless.

※

The Democrats had been out fought, out spent, and out organised in both 2000 and 2004. George W. Bush raised $194 million to Al Gore's $133 million and $375 million to John Kerry's $348 million in 2004. In 2008, however, Barack Obama had raised (including the primaries) $619 million to John McCain's $332 million going into the final stages of the 2008 campaign.*

The advantage was not just in cash terms. The

---

*Christopher Cooper and Laura Meckler, *Wall Street Journal*, October 20, 2008.

campaign had recruited 2 million volunteers by July 2008, a number that was expected to rise to nearer 6 million by Election Day.* In terms of offices and numbers of paid staff the Obama campaign also out-muscled the McCain campaign. Some of the type of campaign infrastructure had been assembled in the John Kerry 2004 campaign but Kerry's campaign had nowhere near the numbers and was nowhere near as well organised.

Through the America Coming Together (ACT) '527 Group' (the legal name for a political action organisation), along with the Kerry campaign itself, voters had been targeted, particularly in swing states such as Ohio (where Karl Rove's organisation was already humming like a new Jaguar car). ACT was funded by George Soros and Peter Lewis – who each ploughed in $20 million – and the union, SEIU, with others.† While ACT and the Kerry campaign experienced coordination difficulties, the Obama campaign was in absolute control of its organisation and wasn't just present in swing states, but all the way across the nation. Every available vote would be taken through voter registration, voter persuasion, mobilisation and getting out the vote. The grassroots spirit echoed Howard Dean's abortive presidential run in 2004, developed Dean's '50-state strategy' and extended the network campaigning of groups such as moveon.org but it was far more focused and effective than any of them.

---

*Brian C Mooney, *Boston Globe*, July 20, 2008.
†Matt Bai, pp.1 8–19.

Obama campaign offices across the nation were adorned with the slogan, RESPECT. EMPOWER. INCLUDE.[*] If Saul Alinsky had written a political campaign organisers' slogan, this could well have been it. A huge amount of time and cash was invested in training field operatives. Their mission, much like Obama's in Altgeld Gardens all those years ago, was replication and empowerment.

They had to identify new recruits, expand the organisation, work out each individual's strengths, entrust and empower them, then watch the voter contacts roll in. In this, the campaign focused on building the skills and capacity of the people who would comprise the campaign infrastructure.

The strategy was to achieve better outcomes by perfecting the process. Volunteers were mainly local and this meant they were better able to connect with the voters they were meeting and talking to over the phone. Underlining its movement characteristics the strategy also worked, not uncontroversially, alongside youth and voter registration organisations such as the Association of Community Organizations for Reform Now (ACORN), the trade unions and a whole series of other community organisations.

It was a campaign that moved beyond the traditional Democratic strongholds of the major metropolitan centres and into suburbs, small towns and the rural districts.

---

[*] Zack Exley, *The New Organizers: What's Really Behind Obama's Ground Game*, http://www.huffingtonpost.com/zack-exley/the-new-organizers-part-1_b_132782.html

Rarely before, if ever, had a Democratic presidential candidate had such a wide-ranging and active campaign.

It made Barack Obama competitive in states where he was not expected to be. Even places like North Dakota were appearing in the potential column for Barack Obama. It also was of great assistance to Democrats running for Congress. His coattails extended down as far as mayoral races. After Barack Obama's victory in South Carolina, one of his most active volunteers, a 37 year-old attorney, Steve Wukela, decided to run for mayor against the incumbent. The Obama campaign that Wukela had played a central role in, had registered 8,000 new voters. Wukela won the race by a single vote.*

The website was the centrepiece of the campaign serving not only to inform, but to organise, recruit and fundraise. Of the campaign's 3 million donors half donated less than $200 with an average donation of $86.† Somehow the campaign managed to mould grassroots campaigning with a central organisational drive. It was both top down and bottom up and that was the root of its success.

❧

If all this was simply about the campaign it would be extremely impressive. But Obama had achieved

---

*Christopher Hayes, *The Nation,* September 1, 2008.
†Christopher Cooper and Laura Meckler, *Wall Street Journal,* October 20, 2008.

something more substantial. Faith groups, the youth vote, community organisations, voter registration organisations, and the millions of volunteers, donors and activists comprise the potential for something greater than simply a campaign. It is the beginning of a movement for change.

One of the tests of his presidency will be his ability to morph Obama '08 into a self-sustaining movement for change based upon a new civic activism and an increased tendency for many, including minorities and young people to vote. His performance as President can be amplified if that transition happens. Social justice in the White House could be matched by social justice in town and city halls on the basis of the gestating and nascent movement for change. Where the right-wing conservative movement seized upon fear and division, Obama has the opportunity to create a political force based on justice that will go beyond his own period of office in the White House.

His agenda, entering the White House in the most trying political times imaginable, combines social investment through widening healthcare coverage, a recasting of America's foreign policy, a new environmentally sensitive economic and energy approach, investment in America's schools and colleges, a new spirit of voluntarism and a tax and economic policy more focused on America's middle-classes. It is an ambitious set of policies in the midst of global financial crisis, the onset of recession and a ballooning Federal deficit. Adversity can induce fundamental change. It did in 1932. It did in 1980. It did in 2001. Change is not always for the better. For Obama, it will have to be.

Already, there are some who are expecting him to fail. David Brooks of *The New York Times* considers his platform to be, 'the Gingrich revolution in reverse and on steroids.'* He pinpoints the cost of the bank bailouts, more stimulus packages, a Keynesian renaissance, the clean energy/jobs programmes, tax cuts and the health-care plan on top of inherited deficits that will lead to an Obama 'over-reach' to which there will be 'backlash.' We'll see. Had David Brooks been around in 1932 he could well have said the same about Franklin Delano Roosevelt. Obama's ability to prioritise and manage his ambitious agenda will determine whether he passes the governance test.

Should he show himself to be a strong President then he has the type of movement behind him that can amplify and expand his achievements. He will need to consider how the movement will survive and prosper once he is in no longer in office. For now, we are at the beginning and the end. It is the beginning of a new chapter of the movement for justice that has manifested itself in so many ways. It is the end of a long wait for the movement that collapsed under its own weight in 1968. Barack Obama, the author of this new chapter, is a culmination of the civil rights movement. He is not its completion. It is now in his hands to take America fur-ther along Martin Luther King's long arc that is bending towards justice.

---

*David Brooks, *The New York Times*, October 14, 2008.

Conclusion

GRANT PARK, CHICAGO. A quarter of a million people assembled to greet President-elect Barack Obama. Roughly the same number gathered to hear Martin Luther King almost half a century before in front of the Lincoln Memorial. Martin Luther King had a dream. That dream drifted from our optimistic sub-conscious to a magnificent reality on November 4, 2008.

Yes, we can! And who can argue? Yes, we can. Yes, we did. Yes, we will. As Barack Obama stood before a crowd, its emotional energy enough to supply renewable energy for a whole generation, a world watched on; amazed but not fazed, rapturous but humble, an ocean of tears swelling and lapping sheer joy onto the shore.

The moment was Barack Obama's. But it was Chicago's too. In these days of renewed belief in collective ownership, it also belonged to the millions of people who fought for this: in history, in Southern cities, plantations, through urban plight and callous neglect; those who donated, volunteered, voted and prayed all played their part.

This was above all America's victory. Yes, America. That country that elected George W. Bush now had elected Barack Obama. Light had sprung from the nadir. Now we, the world, were watching and we were listening again. You are a dream that has too often resembled a nightmare; not this time.

Concluding with the inaugural address in front of the US Capitol, the 2008 campaign can be boiled down to five speeches. The first was in Springfield, where Obama harked back to the spirit of Abraham Lincoln and launched his campaign. Then he reached back to the founding fathers themselves in Philadelphia when he confronted America's racial scars. In Denver, as he made history, he invoked the spirit of Martin Luther King, whose presence is constant in this entire story. Now, in Chicago, he was the story, the next chapter in the long struggle for justice. Fading away was red America and blue America. There was only a United States of America. Barack Obama had told us that way back in 2004. Now, his creed was America's creed and vice versa: *yes, we can.*

There was another story to this victory, one that had slipped by almost without anyone noticing. America has changed. It will no longer be the nasty nation divided along cultural, racial and political lines. Those tricks just don't work anymore. There will no longer be a 'Real America' (Governor Sarah Palin's particularly vindictive contribution to the presidential election, *wink*) or 'Other America' (white America and black America, rural America, small town America, metropolitan America, red America, blue America, elite America and everyday America). That there is all these 'Americas' is the American tale. That is America.

It was only the political power of divisive, populist conservatism that maintained an alternative myth. That myth has been shattered. Those old tricks don't work anymore. As John McCain gave what was a magnanimous and poignant concession speech, there were boos at the mere mention of Barack Obama's name. That resentful America, so long in power in the last half a century, was on the wane.

Instead, America, notwithstanding its current economic travails, is more diverse, educated, liberal, with suburban and metropolitan areas merging, an economy with ideas and expertise at its foundation, and that is very bad news for today's Republican Party. They wrote off this defeat as being down to September's economic crisis. That did have a role to play but was only one of many contributing factors. If they take that as a singular lesson, however, then they will be, events depending, out of power for quite some time to come. Perhaps Governor Sarah Palin will need to be given a run at the presidency in 2012 just to prove to them how out of step they are with this new America. Anger in Arizona will quickly be superseded by despair. A new Republican party will emerge from the ashes, because it has to, but it would seem not for some time yet.

Obama's moderate appeal and his campaign

execution enabled him to win more white voters than either John Kerry or Al Gore did, more religious voters, even those who were frequent church goers, more independent voters, while still capturing the imagination of the traditional Democratic base. This African-American candidate had performed better among those demographics than did the sort of white men that you see on the dollar bill.

There would still be those who saw race as a predominant factor in this election. They too are woefully out of step. Of the miniscule 9 percent of voters who said that race was the most important or one of several important factors in their choice, Barack Obama had a 53 percent to 46 percent margin.*

African-American and Hispanic share of the total vote was up only slightly on 2004; Obama increased the Democrats' margins in those groups making states such as Indiana, Virginia, North Carolina, Nevada and Florida competitive in ways that they may not otherwise have been. Though Barack Obama still had many of the same problems with white, working-class voters that the Democrats have had since Richard Nixon's victory in 1968, his crossover appeal to Independents, upscale whites and others made all the difference.

Now he sits astride a movement for change. His administration will need to contend with the global and domestic crises left for him by the Bush presidency.

Meet the Press, MSNBC, November 9, 2008. John B. Judis, *Los Angeles Times,* November 9, 2008.

He will seek wise counsel and build a bi-partisan coalition, inviting Republicans into his administration to underline this, in order to confront these challenges. He will cut taxes for the vast majority, invest in a green economy, withdraw from Iraq and finally confront the scandal of American healthcare but he will also need to get to grips with a stagnating economy and ballooning Federal deficit. It can be done. Adversity has spawned creativity and opportunity many times before. It will do again.

Of just as much interest is what will now happen to the movement for change. It will be of use to him in office as mass mobilisation to pressure Congress into pursuing his policies. It will help to secure re-election for him. Beyond that, he will have to give it an independent drive and momentum. It can't just be *his* movement for change. It must become America's.

This is his greatest challenge. If he gets this right then he will construct a generation of change rather than simply a term or two. It may seem esoteric or amorphous but the active mobilisation of millions of Americans who can now change their neighbourhoods, their towns, their cities, their states, and inspire further national reform has the potential to be the most powerful force for justice that America has yet seen.

Should he be able to unleash this movement then he will become one of America's greatest Presidents. That is the standard that he has been set. That is what he can achieve. In *un moment tragique* on September 11, 2001, *Le Monde* had declared: '*Nous sommes tous Americains.*'

In time, the world had rejected its new-found solidarity. Now, with the election of Barack Obama, America is searching for that unity again. In these times of change, we are all Americans once again. President Obama, the world is watching and listening. You are the change that we believe in.

Biographical Notes

AUGUST 4, 1961	Barack Hussein Obama II is born in Honolulu, Hawaii to Barack Obama, an economist raised in Alego, Kenya and Ann Dunham, an anthropologist from Wichita, Kansas.
JANUARY 1964	Ann Dunham and Barack Obama Sr divorce in Hawaii though they had been separated since 1962.
1967	Barack Obama and his mother move to Jakarta, Indonesia following her marriage to Lolo Soetoro. Indonesia is in the midst of the unrest that accompanies Suharto's rise to power. Lolo teaches him how to box and he keeps a pet ape.

1971	He returns to Honolulu where he is raised by his maternal grandparents Stanley and Madelyn Dunham. He attends the exclusive Punahou School. His mother returns to Hawaii the following year. His father visits Barack, by now ten years old, and they meet for the final time.
1979	Barack Obama graduates from Punahou School. His mother had returned to Indonesia a couple of years prior to his graduation with his younger half-sister, Maya.
NOVEMBER 4, 1982	Barack Obama Sr dies in a car accident in Nairobi, Kenya.
1983	Graduates from Columbia University in New York with a degree in political science (specialising in international relations.) Obama had transferred there after a couple of years at the Occidental College in Los Angeles.
1985	Moves to Chicago after a frustrating couple of years in New York. He becomes a director of the Developing Communities Project where he works in communities on Chicago's South Side including Altgeld Gardens.

1988	Enters Harvard Law School. In 1990, he is elected the first black president of the *Harvard Law Review*. That gains him national attention and leads to a book deal that eventually results in *Dreams from My Father*.
JUNE 1989	Meets Michelle Robinson while on a summer placement at the Chicago law firm, Sidley Austin.
1991	Returns to Chicago. Joins Project Vote in 1992 and registers 150,000 African-American voters.
OCTOBER 1992	Barack Obama and Michelle Robinson marry.
1993	Joins Chicago law firm, Miner, Barnhill, and Galland. Also teaches constitutional law at the University of Chicago Law School.
1995	*Dreams from My Father* published.
NOVEMBER 7, 1995	Ann Dunham Soetoro, Barack's mother, dies of ovarian and uterine cancers.
1996	Elected as State Senator for Illinois' 13th District, succeeding Alice Palmer in controversial circumstances.

1999	Malia Obama, Michelle and Barack's first daughter is born.
MARCH 21, 2000	Loses the primary for the House of Representatives Illinois 1st District to the incumbent, Congressman Bobby Rush, by a huge two to one margin; a campaign he later regrets running in.
2001	Natasha (Sasha) Obama is born.
OCTOBER 2, 2002	Delivers speech against the Iraq War describing the invasion as 'rash'.
JANUARY 2003	Announces his candidacy for the US Senate and employs David Axelrod as a campaign consultant. He wins the campaign by over 20 points against Dan Hynes in March 2004.
27 JULY 2004	Delivers the keynote speech to the 2004 Democratic Convention launching himself onto the national scene and laying the path for a presidential run.

NOVEMBER 2, 2004 — Elected US Senator for Illinois defeating Alan Keyes by 70 per cent to 27 per cent, the largest margin in Illinois history. His time as Senator features a number of bi-partisan initiatives including nuclear proliferation and government transparency. He also became a member of the Foreign Relations Committee, serving under the Chairmanship of Senator Joe Biden for a period of time.

OCTOBER 2006 — *The Audacity of Hope* published.

FEBRUARY 10, 2007 — Announces his candidacy for President of the United States of America in front of the Old State Capitol Building in Springfield, Illinois; the location where Abraham Lincoln delivered his 'A house divided cannot stand' speech in 1858. His main opponents would be Senators Hillary Clinton and John Edwards.

DECEMBER 8, 2007 — Daytime talk-show queen, Oprah Winfrey, endorses Barack Obama.

JANUARY 3, 2008	Wins a comfortable victory in the Iowa caucus with his main rival, Hillary Clinton, in third place. He declares: 'This was the moment when the improbable beat what Washington always said was inevitable.' Five days later, Hillary Clinton fights back with a win in New Hampshire.
FEBRUARY 5, 2008	Wins more states and more delegates than Hillary Clinton on Super Tuesday. He goes on to record 12 straight victories in February before losing the Texas and Ohio primaries on March 4th.
MARCH 18, 2008	Delivers his 'A more perfect union speech' in Philadelphia addressing America's racial history and present.
APRIL 29, 2008	Renounces his former pastor, Reverend Jeremiah Wright, for anti-American and inflammatory comments.
JUNE 3, 2008	Clinches the Democratic nomination and Hillary Clinton suspends her campaign and endorses him four days later.

JULY 24, 2008	World trip includes a visit to Berlin where he delivers a speech to a crowd of 200,000. Some label the moment as 'presumptuous'.
AUGUST 23, 2008	Announces Delaware Senator Joe Biden as his running-mate.
AUGUST 27, 2008	Watched by 84,000 people at Mile High Stadium in Denver and a further 38 million on television, Barack Obama accepts the Democratic nomination for President, the first African-American to do so.
SEPTEMBER 14, 2008	Lehman Brothers investment back goes into administration initiating an intense global financial crisis. Senator McCain, Obama's Republican rival, 'suspends' his campaign on September 24th in response to a proposed $700 billion financial bail-out but Barack Obama's calm handling of the crisis is notable and becomes a turning point in the campaign.
SEPTEMBER TO OCTOBER 2008	Obama's performances in the presidential debate are warmly received and he builds a poll lead that was to prove insurmountable.

OCTOBER 19, 2008   Republican Colin Powell, former Secretary of State under George W. Bush and Chairman of the Joint Chiefs of Staff, endorses Barack Obama.

NOVEMBER 2, 2008   Madelyn Dunham dies from cancer at the age of 86. Barack Obama takes time off from the campaign trail to visit her just a few days previously. She casts her absentee ballot for her grandson before her death.

NOVEMBER 4, 2008   Elected President. His victory speech is watched live by somewhere in the region of 250,000 in Grant Park, Chicago and hundreds of millions worldwide.

Sources: *Milestones: Barack Obama* (*The New York Times*), Wikipedia, *Change We Can Believe In* (Obama '08), *Dreams from My Father* (Barack Obama).

Acknowledgements

FIRST AND FOREMOST I MUST THANK Rosemarie Hudson, who commissioned this book at Arcadia. It was obvious that things were going to work when we hit the gin and tonics soon into our first meeting. Gary, Andy and Daniela have also been instrumental in making this project a reality. A special mention should also go to Barrie Clement who first suggested that Rosemarie should get in contact with me, and without whom this would not have happened.

I have met so many people who have illuminated and inspired me during this incredible journey. Linda Randle is a force of nature and my only hope is that I have captured her personality in this book because she is infectious, intelligent and brilliant. Both Linda and Rod Smith were great company in Denver and helped me in so many ways, not least in getting a great seat for the Mile High Stadium speech.

Paulette Edwards at Project 18, Bernadette Williams,

Shawana Walton, Gail Reed, Kim and so many others who I met in Altgeld Gardens and who are the voices that we hear in the Chicago section of the book all showed me patience and understanding. I wish I could have spent even more time hanging out in AG. Again, I hope that I have done them justice. Loretta Augustine-Herron provided me with deep understanding of Altgeld Gardens in the 1980s and how it changed over time. Thank you to Alderman Toni Preckwinkle and Alderman Anthony Beale for taking time out of their busy schedule to speak to me. Also, Annie Estabrook at the Harold Washington Library in Chicago went way beyond the call of duty and gave me excellent background into Chicago's Latino communities.

Al Kindle taught me more about Chicago politics in conversation than a thousand articles and books could have done. It's people like Al who have made this happen. David Lammy MP kindly lent me his knowledge of the man and his own global political perspective.

A special note of thanks must go to Hamza Elahi who proofread, challenged and considerably improved the text. I am looking forward to reading his first novel. Paul Roe, whose encyclopaedic knowledge of the Kennedys and 1960s America was so helpful in the book's first chapter requires a special mention. The comments and support from Steve and Julia George who cast their journalistic gaze over key portions of the book were invaluable as was their friendship and expertise. All errors and omissions are mine.

Finally, so many people have given me so much

support during the course of this book but I must mention them in no particular order: Steve (A and E), Becca, Reverend Simon, Vidhya, Mark (who has many names), Teresa, Jessica, Richard and Ed.

Thank you all.

Anthony Painter
November 5, 2008

Bibliography

A SPECIAL MENTION should be made of David Mendell's biography of Barack Obama as well as *Dreams from My Father* and *The Audacity of Hope*. I would strongly recommend reading all three: this book would simply not have been possible without them.

Alinsky, Saul. *Rules for Radicals: A Pragmatic Primer for Realistic Radicals*. New York: Vintage, 1989 edition.

Bai, Matt. *The Argument: Billionaires, Bloggers and the Battle to Remake Democratic Politics*. New York: Penguin Press, 2007.

Caro, Robert A. *The Years of Lyndon Johnson: The Path to Power*. New York: Vintage Books, 1991 edition.

Caro, Robert A. *The Years of Lyndon Johnson: Means of Ascent*. New York: Vintage Books, 1991.

Caro, Robert A. *The Years of Lyndon Johnson: Master of the Senate*. New York: Vintage Books, 2003.

Clavel, Pierre and Wiewel, Wim. *Harold Washington and the Neighbourhoods: Progressive City Government in Chicago, 1983–87.* Piscataway: Rutger University Press, 1991.

Edsall, Thomas Byrne and Edsall, Mary D. *Chain Reaction: The Impact of Race, Rights and Taxes on American Politics.* New York: Norton, 1992.

Frady, Marshall. *Martin Luther King, Jr.: A Life.* New York: Penguin Books, 2002.

Frank, Thomas. *What's the Matter with Kansas?* New York: Owl Books, 2005 edition.

Graubard, Stephen. *The Presidents: The Transformation of the American Presidency from Theodore Roosevelt to George W. Bush.* London: Penguin Books, 2004.

Hacker, Jacob S. *The Great Risk Shift: The Assault on American Jobs, Families, Health Care and Retirement and How You Can Fight Back.* New York: Oxford University Press, 2006.

Harrington, Michael, *The Other America: Poverty in the United States.* Baltimore: Penguin Books, 1962.

Judia, John B. and Teixeira, Ruy, *The Emerging Democratic Majority.* New York: Scribner, 2002.

Kearns Goodwin, Doris. *Lyndon Johnson and the American Dream.* New York: St Martin's Griffin, 1991 edition.

Luntz, Dr Frank. *Words that Work: It's Not What You Say, It's What People Hear.* New York: Hyperion Books, 2007.

Mendell, David. *Obama: From Promise to Power.* New York: Amistad, 2007.

Micklethwait, John and Wooldridge, Adrian. *The Right Nation: Why America is Different*. London: Penguin Books, 2004.

Miller, Alton. *Harold Washington: The Mayor, the Man*. Santa Monica: Bonus Books, 1989.

Moore, James and Slater, Wayne. *The Architect: Karl Rove and the Dream of Absolute Power*. New York: Three Rivers Press, 2006.

Newfield, Jack. *RFK: A Memoir*. New York: Nation Books, 2003 edition.

Obama '08. *Change We Can Believe In: Barack Obama's Plan to Renew America's Promise*. New York: Three Rivers Press, 2008.

Obama, Barack. *Dreams from My Father*. New York: Canongate, 2008 edition.

Obama, Barack. *The Audacity of Hope: Thoughts on Reclaiming the American Dream*. New York: Crown Publishers, 2006.

Palermo, Joseph A. *In His Own Right: The Political Odyssey of Senator Robert F. Kennedy*. New York: Columbia University Press, 2001.

Perlstein, Rick. *Nixonland: The Rise of a President and the Fracturing of America*. New York: Scribner, 2008.

Regnery, Alfred S. *Upstream: The Ascendance of American Conservatism*. New York: Threshold Editions, 2008.

Reich, Robert B. *Supercapitalism: The Transformation of Business, Democracy and Everyday Life*. New York: Alfred A. Knopf, 2007.

Royko, Mike. *Boss: Richard J. Daley of Chicago.* New York: Plume Books, 1988 edition.

Steele, Shelby. *A Bound Man: Why We are Excited by Obama and Why He Can't Win.* New York: Ibooks, 2007.

Travis, Dempsey J. *Harold Washington: The People's Mayor.* Chicago: Urban Research Press, 1989.

Washington, James M (editor). *A Testament of Hope: The Essential Writings of Martin Luther King, Jr.* San Francisco: HarperCollins, 1991.

West, Cornel. *Democracy Matters: Winning the Fight Against Imperialism.* New York: Penguin Books, 2004.

West, Cornel. *Race Matters.* New York: Vintage Books, 2001 edition.